SARI TO SARONG

SARI TO
Five hundred years of Indian
SARONG
and Indonesian textile exchange

Robyn Maxwell

■ national gallery of **australia**

Produced by the Publications Department
of the National Gallery of Australia

nga.gov.au
The National Gallery of Australia is a Federal Government Agency.

Designer: Kirsty Morrison
Printer: Inprint

Cataloguing-in-Publication-data

Maxwell, Robyn.
Sari to sarong: 500 years of Indian and Indonesian textile exchange.
Bibliography.

   ISBN 0 642 54113 2

   1. Textile crafts - India - Exhibitions. 2. Textile crafts - Indonesia
   Exhibitions. 3. Indonesia - Civilization - Indic influences.
   I. National Gallery of Australia. II. Title.

   746.0954

This catalogue was published on the occasion of the exhibition
Sari to Sarong: 500 years of Indian and Indonesian textile exchange
National Gallery of Australia, Canberra   11 July – 6 October 2003

National Gallery of Australia textile conservators
   Bronwyn Cosgrove
   Micheline Ford
   Jael Muspratt
   Solitaire Sani
   Charis Tyrrel
   Debbie Ward
   Jane Wild

Conservation volunteers
   Teresa Duhigg
   Gudrun Genee
   Helen Hanley

National Gallery of Australia Department of Asian Art staff
   Carol Cains
   Caroline Davies
   Ben Divall
   Charlotte Galloway
   Robyn Maxwell

Asian Art interns
   Lucie Folan
   Angela Silk

Distributed in Australia by
Thames and Hudson
11 Central Boulevard Business Park
Port Melbourne, Victoria 3207

Distributed in the United Kingdom by
Thames and Hudson
181A High Holborn
London WC1V 7QX, UK

Distributed in the United States of America by
University of Washington Press
1326 Fifth Avenue, Ste 555
Seattle, WA 98101-2604

(cover) Coromandel coast, India
Traded to Bali, Indonesia
Heirloom hanging [*palampore*] late 17th century (detail)
cotton, natural dyes, mordants; mordant painting
164.0 x 106.0 cm
Gift of Cecilia Ng in memory of Anthony Forge
2002.152

CONTENTS

I can still vividly recall my first encounter with the textiles of India and Indonesia. As a result of the major reconfiguration of the Gallery's permanent displays that occurred six months after my arrival in Canberra from Dublin, the Asian collection moved to the spacious Lower Galleries. The curators and conservators had worked with energy and flair to show the national collection of Asian art to its best advantage. Recognising the need to demonstrate the diversity and the unique qualities of Canberra's holdings, the displays for that March 1998 opening integrated sculpture, ceramics, works on paper, installations and paintings, along with the Gallery's great strength in the Asian art field — textiles.

I was captivated by the richness and beauty of the great variety of textiles, largely from South and Southeast Asia. I was immediately convinced, as the founding Director of the National Gallery, James Mollison, had been before me, that for the Southeast Asian region, textiles are a truly exciting, innovative, diverse and alive art form. Delighted and intrigued by this surprisingly rich part of the Gallery's collection, I became determined to continue James Mollison's vision to collect and showcase the region's pre-eminent art form in depth. We would maintain and enhance the strong presence of textiles in our permanent displays of Asian art, and therefore show to the world the Gallery's confidence in this important art form of our geographical region.

The major 1990 exhibition *Tradition, Trade and Transformation: Textiles of Southeast Asia* had placed the Gallery's collection on the international stage, consolidated by an important loan exhibition to the Asia Society Galleries in New York. Recent developments have continued to underline the Gallery's international standing in the field of Asian textiles. The acquisition, by purchase and gift, of a substantial part of one of the world's most renowned private holdings of Indonesian textiles was greeted with great excitement and approval in Australia and internationally. The works from the collection of Robert J Holmgren and Anita E Spertus added to the strengths of the Gallery's established holdings, especially from south Sumatra and Sulawesi.

This exhibition, *Sari to Sarong: 500 years of Indian and Indonesian textile exchange*, provides an opportunity to show some of the highlights of our collection. It has also provided the impetus to conserve and display some of the numerous gifts that the Gallery has attracted over the years. To this end the Gallery's talented textile conservators, led by Debbie Ward, have been developing new methods to research and safely present the textiles, some centuries old, to their best advantage. A selection of works from the most significant of these benefactions — those received from Michael Abbott QC and Mary Abbott — is exhibited in *Sari to Sarong*. In particular, an important group of Indian textiles, traded to Indonesia across the centuries, some dating from as early as the 14th century, are a key focus of the exhibition. The Indian cottons and silks are shown beside a great variety of Indonesian textiles whose form and design they inspired.

The Gallery's Senior Curator of Asian Art, Robyn Maxwell, has a well-established reputation in the field of Asian textiles and has been involved in the development of the collection since its inception in 1979. Her knowledge and experience provided an original approach to the works in the collection. A brilliant, inspiring and indefatigable colleague, in *Sari to Sarong* Robyn Maxwell has drawn fascinating visual and historical links between India and Indonesia. These have informed and inspired some of the region's greatest works of art. In creating this splendid introduction to the history and art of India and Indonesia, she and fellow Asian art curators Charlotte Galloway and Carol Cains

have been supported by the Gallery's dedicated professional staff. I am grateful to each and every one for their determined efforts to achieve an exhibition and catalogue worthy of our splendid collections.

A significant financial gift offered to the Gallery by our Council member and benefactor Mrs Lyn Williams AM has been dedicated to the support of the exhibition *Sari to Sarong* and this publication. She is owed a debt of gratitude for this contribution, but especially for her role as the main agent within the National Gallery of Australia Council, offering support for our efforts to make vital and expensive acquisitions to enhance the Asian textiles collection, which had its inception while her late husband, the celebrated artist Fred Williams OBE, was a member of the Gallery's Council.

It gives me great pleasure to end with words from Mrs Lyn Williams:

Indonesia is our nearest neighbour. Its textiles are one of its most treasured and significant cultural expressions. As we learn to understand and appreciate them, so we will our Asian neighbours.

The depth and richness of the National Gallery of Australia's great collection of these works gives us that opportunity, as indicated in this exhibition and its supporting publication.

On the other hand we may simply enjoy them for themselves as arresting and beautiful works of art.

Brian Kennedy
Director
National Gallery of Australia

Between the vast subcontinent of India and the sprawling archipelago of Indonesia, across wide oceans and through narrow straits, ideas, technologies and objects have intersected and interacted for perhaps 2000 years. *Sari to Sarong: 500 years of Indian and Indonesian textile exchange* explores the range and depth of those encounters — sometimes strikingly obvious, often subtle and enigmatic — as they are revealed in the textile arts of Indonesia.

The impact of the great philosophies and religions of India on the cultures of the Southeast Asian region has been much discussed, especially in relation to architecture and sculpture. In particular the relationships between India and Indonesia during the first millennium of the present era have long been a source of fascination for archaeologists and art historians: their attention has focused on the impressive ruins of Java and the vibrant arts of Hindu Bali. These are the clearest reminders of ancient connections between two large and culturally diverse countries, but the exchanges between India and Indonesia have been multifaceted, with subtleties and surprises abounding. Together the remains of the great monuments and tiny shrines provide a lasting and tangible testament to the extent of the spread of Buddhism and Hinduism from the Indian subcontinent, especially to the ancient central realms of the Indonesian archipelago. The textile arts of these classical periods of Hinduism and Buddhism have not survived, except as they are depicted in the stone and metal images from those early kingdoms. Only in the arts of Bali, where the Hindu religion is still vital, do textiles continue to combine functions and forms that can be traced to Indic sources.

(opposite) Paminggir people
Lampung, south Sumatra, Indonesia
Woman's ceremonial skirt [*tapis*] 19th century (detail)
cotton, silk, mica pieces, gold thread; embroidery, appliqué,
warp ikat 131.0 x 118.0 cm
Acquired through gift and purchase from the Collection of
Robert J. Holmgren and Anita Spertus, New York, 2000 2000.933

India and Indonesia arguably sustain the richest and most varied textile cultures in the world — traditions that have been constantly evolving since prehistoric times. In both regions textiles have long been very significant art forms, sometimes interchangeable with, often equal to and frequently surpassing achievements in works of art in other media. Most importantly it has been in the textile arts that the exchanges between the Indian subcontinent and the islands of the Indonesian archipelago have been most gloriously displayed during the past 500 years. The influence of India on Indonesian textiles has not, however, been limited to the periods and regions where Indic cultures were most firmly implanted over a thousand years ago. For instance, while there are no ancient temple ruins on the eastern island of Lembata, the influence of India is still today brilliantly displayed on the women's locally woven cotton skirts. Balinese textiles also resonate with Indian themes; these are not only evident in temples and shrines, but in the meanings that they have outside the Hindu rites, for the Balinese uses of textiles have many parallels with those associated with the ancestral rites of eastern Indonesia, where the great Indic religions — Hinduism and Buddhism — had little impact on ancient autochthonous Indonesian beliefs and practices.

Perhaps surprisingly, textiles from Indonesian cultures where Islam has long been supreme also retain memories of earlier Indian iconography and meaning. These can be observed most clearly in the textiles and costumes associated with the ceremonies and regalia of the court centres, long the patrons and consumers of the finest arts. While Islam has almost exclusively been the religious orientation of most coastal principalities commanding the key harbours and estuaries of the archipelago, from the late 15th century onwards it was also embraced by the rulers of the great Javanese feudal empire of Mataram and its successors. The legitimacy of rulers, however, often depends on the display of ancient symbols of power and rank — the heritage of Indian models of kingship and hierarchy. The parasols of rank were not only held high above the descendants of the great Javanese empires of Sailendra and Majapahit but they also sheltered the princes of bustling international entrepot of east Sumatra. They are associated with the cremations of Balinese princes and with the funerals of Buginese sultans.

The many kingdoms of Indonesia were based on the control of wealth, and particularly of trade. The natural wealth of the archipelago — its aromatic spices, resins and woods, its mineral resources and marine harvests — moved through the ports and palaces of the archipelago's many city-states and out into the international theatre of commerce. Kingdoms and principalities, large and small, mushroomed around the major ports and river estuaries controlling the entrepot trade. Foreign and local ships plied between India and the western reaches of the Indian Ocean, Southeast Asia and on to China and Japan in the east. Vessels of various sizes and flag pushed deep into the archipelago and up the great rivers following the natural riches and agricultural produce of Indonesia.

It was, however, India's early supremacy in textile arts that provided the crucial element in the quest for Indonesian spices. The most desirable items of exchange in the vigorous and long-lasting trade for Indonesian primary produce were Indian textiles. Over the centuries hundreds of thousands of metres of Indian cloth — predominantly cotton but also silk — were shipped into the Indonesian archipelago. The fabrics ranged from undyed and monochrome bales of sturdy weaves to exquisitely painted cottons and intricately tie-dyed silks. Single lengths of the most expensive and desirable types rated very highly in the barter for primary produce and for gold and silver. Until the late 18th century the trade in textiles — by various Indonesian and Indian communities, by Arab and other Islamic sailors, by Dutch, English and other European commercial companies and governments — took Indian cloth into both cosmopolitan and remote districts of the archipelago.

The control of these exotic textiles was always in the hands of the powerful and the wealthy. By the 16th century the newest participants in this international trade were the Europeans; arriving relatively late on the scene following the discovery of the sea route to India around the Horn of Africa in 1497–98 by Portuguese adventurer Vasco da Gama, they entered the Asian market with a vengeance. First the Portuguese, then the Spanish, Dutch and English were among those most anxious to secure a significant portion of the spice market. In Indonesia today the visible signs of these endeavours are the remains of fortifications scattered across the archipelago, such as Portuguese strongholds on the islands of Flores and Solor in eastern Indonesia, and the impressive English Fort Marlborough in the west Sumatran province of Bengkulu. The evidence of the ultimate supremacy of the Dutch is everywhere throughout the archipelago, the earlier monopolies of their United East India Company (*Vereenigde*

Oost-Indische Compagnie) paving the way for the establishment of the Netherlands East Indies colony in the 19th century.

The reminders of the dramatic shift of the cloth trade to European control can also be found in the great textile-producing centres of India. Not satisfied in merely shipping the Indian textiles to the east for spices and profit, the English and Dutch companies set up trading posts in Gujarat in west India and along the length of the eastern Coromandel coast to amass the regular quantities of textiles needed to engage in the barter exchanges, and to edge out their Asian and European rivals alike.

This tussle for supremacy and the wresting of control from Asian rulers and traders is the basis for many histories of pre-colonial South and Southeast Asia, for the Europeans were only the latest players in textile commerce, which already stretched back over a millennium. They adopted the products and tactics of their Asian and Arab predecessors and competitors — purchasing textiles in India for exchange in the great Indonesian entrepots of Aceh, Malacca, Banten, Makassar and Batavia (Jakarta), and at the source in Ternate and Maluku in the east, and in pepper-rich Lampung in south Sumatra. The Europeans too learned from bitter experience that different markets throughout Indonesia had particular and preferred tastes in Indian cloth, colour and design. They were to discover that the Indian artisans were not only the masters of technical skills, especially the arts of colour-fast dyeing, but also experts in adapting to market demands. By the 17th century Europe itself had fallen under the spell of Indian textiles; superfine muslin, brightly painted floral chintz and whimsical silk embroideries were such a rage that their threat to local European textiles industries evoked a raft of legal proscriptions on the import of Indian cotton textiles.

Of course, the Indonesians and the Europeans were not the only eager recipients of the products of India's renowned textile skills. In fact it is somewhat ironic that the oldest decorated Indian textiles to survive are those made for foreign trade — found at ancient Buddhist sites along the Silk Road in Central Asia, in excavations of mediaeval port cities in the Middle East, and in the local treasuries of island Indonesia. While these can in no way be considered typical of Indian textile production across thousands of years, they provide glimpses of the technical prowess of Indian artisans that has been legendary since ancient times.

However, the relatively large numbers, the rich variety and the generally excellent condition of the Indian textiles surviving in Indonesia are an indication of the huge volume of trade into the Spice Islands in pre-colonial times. They also demonstrate the eclectic and sophisticated taste and passion for beautiful textiles that still amaze travellers and collectors of Indonesian cloth; even those very familiar with historical Indonesian textiles are sometimes surprised by a new form, type or technique not previously recorded in the great European collections of the 19th and 20th centuries. It was this enthusiasm for textiles — local and exotic — that fuelled the barter in Indian cloth over centuries.

Unlike the fragments of early Indian textiles that have been recovered elsewhere, a substantial number of those that have survived in Indonesia are largely intact. Metres of decorative Indian cloth, some now scientifically dated to as early as the 14th century, long before the escalation of trade following European intervention, have endured the hot tropical conditions of equatorial Asia, the attacks of insects and rodents, the documented periods of war and social unrest, and the considerable displacements of populations in historical times in some of the most remote locations in Indonesia. The reason for the surprising preservation of these clothes can be found in the admiration for and in many cases the veneration of fine textiles in most Indonesian cultures.

Textiles are arguably the most enduring and culturally significant art form throughout the Indonesian region. A wide range of decorative techniques, including supplementary thread-weaving, pattern dyeing, embroidery, appliqué, batik and pigment painting, has long been practised throughout the archipelago. Anthropologists and historians have documented the ancient yet continuing importance of textiles in ritual and exchange. Their presence and significance in every form of ritual in great part accounts for the efforts made to create and preserve objects of outstanding beauty and technical complexity.

Rare and expensive textiles, both local and imported, became more than just representations of wealth: the cloths were identified with their aristocratic owners and were symbols of their power and status, both temporal and spiritual. For a clan chieftain or shaman of a small community in the far-flung islands of eastern Indonesia, and for the feudal lord of a Java royal court, Indian textiles became part of their possessions and identity as rulers — through apparel, furnishing or regalia. This was particularly the case with the Indian imports: the importance and meaning of the exotic textiles shifted from essential currency to sacred heirloom. In fact the loss of control of sacred regalia and treasured heirlooms, or their deterioration, was often taken as a sign of a failed leader or an impending disaster.

The result of this extraordinary care is an amazing archive for both Indonesian and Indian textile history, since there are no counterparts of the same age and design back in India and, to this point in time, there are no Indonesian textiles of similar antiquity known to have survived. The textile techniques used to create these Indian historical textiles are few, representing a small part of the enormous range of decorative techniques used currently and in the past by Indian artisans. The luminous silk *patola* from Gujarat in west India, patterned by a complex double ikat-resist

technique, were much admired but were always the smallest portion of the shipments to Indonesia. Produced both in west India and along the Coromandel coast, the decorative cottons (known in India by terms such as *kalamkari* and in the international trade as *sarasa* and *chintz*) were created by the painting and block-printing of different metallic mordants onto cloth that was then immersed in India's famous turkey-red dyes.

There was clearly enormous variety in the designs on the mordant-patterned cotton textiles imported into Indonesia. These range from quintessentially Indian motifs and styles to shapes and features that are only known in Indonesian contexts. They include 6-metre *sari* lengths and smaller formats that relate closely to the modern Indonesian *sarong*. While some of the imported textiles found in Indonesia display the imagery of domestic Indian art and religion, including scenes from the great Ramayana epic, most do not. It seems that the Indian ability and flexibility to adapt to customer demands meant that the various tastes of a diverse Indonesian market could be and was readily satisfied.

That this was not the case with the silk *patola* is not surprising since the complex double ikat technique has tended to constrain designs to a limited repertoire; while exciting recent discoveries of previously unknown *patola* patterns have caused art historians to review this range, it will certainly remain much smaller than that of the cotton chintzes produced by the more flexible painting and block-printing methods. On the other hand, while the importance of the brilliant silk *patola* in Indonesian cultures has long been recognised, the significance of the patterned cottons has been greatly underestimated. Because of the similarity of some cotton designs to the popular *patola*, art historians have often failed to differentiate between cheaper cotton versions of the double ikat and the many and varied, often much more ancient, types of Indian cotton textiles that have been preserved across Indonesia for centuries.

The patterns and styles of these prestigious imported textiles, very different in appearance and technique from local weaves, have long been a source of inspiration for talented artisans throughout the archipelago. While this appears especially to be the case with textiles required in a palace or temple, Indian designs and motifs have been incorporated into the textiles of many smaller village communities from one end of the island chain to the other. From the remote mountainous districts of the large islands of Sumatra and Sulawesi (Celebes) to places far removed today from the main axis of communications (for example, Flores and Sumba in the east), the appeal of Indian textiles traded into those parts in past centuries has never waned.

As the Indian counterparts became rarer and more fragile, it is probable that the process of replication accelerated as attempts to secure the essence of sacred regalia became increasingly urgent. Applying a great range of decorative techniques and materials — indigenous, naturalised and freshly imported — the women of Indonesia created new motifs and designs that emulated the Indian models. This was sometimes achieved with fabulous similitude, although more often the different textures, fibres, dyes and techniques, combined with unique local readings of the original motif or pattern, resulted in subtle transpositions of elements. In some cultures the symbolic meaning, even the essence of the treasured heirlooms, was deemed to have been recreated on Indonesian cloth.

There are, however, fundamental differences in the cosmological and social milieu surrounding the creation of significant textiles in Indonesia and the production of even the most expensive and complex of the Indian textiles for trade. It was and continues almost exclusively to be women who create hand-loom textiles in Indonesia. In India, however, the division along gender lines between the production of textiles for domestic use and for trade, and between palace and village, has a long history. The dominance of men in commercial enterprises is obvious in the textile production — of both the *patola* silks and the hand-drawn and hand-printed cottons — for international trade. Thus, while it is likely that even the oldest Indian textiles found in Indonesia were woven and decorated by men, beautiful or culturally significant textiles — old or new, made in any part of Indonesia — are women's art. They are not only fully recognised as the work of women, but also their inherent femaleness is an important aspect of their ritual potency. They complement men's skills and arts, essential for balance in the realms of nature and the supernatural. This pairing of male and female elements ensures the presence and prominence of fine textiles at every ritual in the lifecycle of the individual and in the annual calendar of communal activities in village and court throughout Indonesia.

While the many Indian textiles arriving on Indonesian shores were items of commerce, the status of those that have survived the intervening centuries has clearly changed. Despite their exotic nature, the foreign heirlooms have been absorbed into the hierarchies of Indonesian society and art. In particular the Indian treasures are firmly placed in the female sphere of ceremonial activities; in many instances they have been awarded the highest rank in regional systems of textile value, ahead of the finest and most prestigious local products created by the most skilled Indonesian textile artists.

The exchanges with India were one important dimension of Indonesia's long involvement in sea voyages and maritime activities. The ancestors of modern Indonesians had migrated in prehistoric times from the region of today's southern China through Taiwan, down through the islands of the Philippines and into the arc of the Indonesian archipelago. Some of their number would continue out into the Pacific and on to New Zealand, while others would cross another vast ocean to Madagascar. Their shared Austronesian culture and language placed great significance on maritime skills and symbolism. The ancestors literally and metaphorically arrived by ship or boat, the shapes of the great clan house echoing the lines of those vessels. Cave paintings in New Guinea depict ancestors with boats, while huge symbolic stone canoes with elaborately carved prows are laid out in the central plazas of ancestral villages in Tanimbar. Many of the great bronze drums imported into the archipelago from the Dong Son region of north Vietnam in the early centuries of the present era are embellished with images of long boats with their crews in feathered headdress. These images and even their style of depiction have continued to resonate throughout Indonesian art to the present era. They are also evidence that Indonesia's fascination with exotic trade objects began long ago.

Throughout the archipelago ship imagery and terminology are not only applied to objects, but also often to social structures, cultural rites and cosmological concepts. Communities are ordered as if the crew of a ship, led by the village 'captain' and 'pilot'. Marriage processions float in ship-like formations from the dwelling of the groom's family to his bride's home. On Sumba, tall masts tied with textile sails are also symbolically erected on huge slabs of stone as they are dragged great distances by villagers to create the tombs of clan chieftains. During construction, the central clan house also flies a textile 'sail'. On such occasions the ship symbolism is closely associated with the changes in status — social and spiritual — that occur throughout a person's life.

These voyages of the soul are marked by ceremonies, the size of which depends largely on the stature and achievements of the individual and the rank of his or her family. The most important of these transitions is from life to death when, in the ancient ancestral belief systems of Indonesia, the prominent dead will take their places in the next life as significant ancestors, able to intercede and interfere in the affairs of the living. It is in this crucial journey that the ship is linked most symbolically.

It is not surprising then that an important recurring image in Indonesian mortuary art is the ship or boat. Wooden ship-shaped coffins enclose the bones of the dead in Borneo and appear on prehistoric sarcophagi in south Sumatra. Although this association with death is particularly striking in ancestral cultures, ship imagery is also associated with rituals of the lifecycle in Indonesian cultures where the great world religions of Hinduism, Islam and Christianity have made considerable impact. There the conspicuous presence of the ship motif at the many rites of passage that mark those points of transition is a reminder of the ancestry of the peoples of the Indonesian archipelago and of their close relationship with the sea and with maritime endeavours. However, these ceremonies are as much associated with the passages of the living as they are with the last voyages of the dead.

Of all art forms, it is textiles that most clearly display striking ship images at such rites of passage. In the Lampung region of south Sumatra, the ship motifs are particularly powerful and pervasive, appearing on a range of textile forms and materials, created by the whole gamut of popular local techniques. From interlaced fibres to burnt pokerwork incising, from mats to baskets for the essential ingredients for betel-nut chewing, ships appear on all manner of textiles across this strategically placed region of south Sumatra. Situated on the Sunda and Malacca straits at the crossroads of more than a millennium of international trade, especially between the eastern Spice islands, India and the West, the region's wealth was also derived from primary produce, particularly pepper and gold.

These international engagements provided a sound economic base and rich sources of imagery for the elaborate ceremonies at which dramatic textiles have long been an essential feature. At these, women wore splendid *tapis* — cylindrical skirts with the often sombre and mysterious warp ikat illuminated by brilliant embroidered bands of exotic silk and gold thread. These skirts display images associated with major rites of passage; alongside the often dominant ship motifs peopled with figures in flaming headdress are enigmatic human images outstretched on platforms, punts or biers. The occasional presence of huge bird figures suggests another popular set of transition imagery in the pan-Malay world: bridal carriages display huge hornbill 'prows' and young princes are carried to their circumcisions atop gold-covered bird-shaped floats.

The ship images are, however, most prominent on specially woven multifunctional textiles that feature prominently at the many ceremonies that celebrate the individual's journey through the lifecycle. These textiles are not items of clothing, yet from birth to death the small square *tampan* are conspicuously present at important rituals. Woven in series in handspun cotton on a simple back-tension loom, the designs usually appear in dark red and brown floating wefts, with details and borders in indigo-blue and turmeric yellow, against a white background.

The *tampan* appears to have been omnipresent at all rites of passage in parts of Lampung. A young baby is laid upon a *tampan* when formally introduced to his maternal grandparents, while his father's family brings gifts wrapped in *tampan* squares. The transitions from child to adult and from single to married are also marked by the display of these ship-emblazoned textiles. On the cusp of adulthood a boy sits at his circumcision on a *tampan*, while another covers his ceremonial meal. At marriage negotiations between the extended families, *tampan* again cover gifts and food, and the bridal couple themselves are seated at their

wedding on small shipcloths. Even when eloping, a young man brings his fiancée gifts wrapped in *tampan* squares and leaves a token shipcloth in their wake. It is wrapped around its male counterpart — the metal sword or lance — to be carried in marriage procession. In each event the *tampan* facilitates the passage while protecting the protagonists. Its association with death may have become less pronounced with cultural and religious changes over recent centuries.

The ship images on these *tampan* take many forms, from the simple curved lines of a canoe to elaborately masted sailing vessels. Their passengers vary also. On the more stylised Kalianda textiles from the southern-most districts of the province, small ambiguous figures, animals, boats, trees, shrines and pavilions are stacked towards the bird-filled heavens, the curving prow aligned with the upturned eaves of architectural structures. Linear features are everywhere embellished with decorative hooks and spirals.

On many *tampan* from the Pasisir coastal plains of southern Lampung single imposing vessels dominate; their decks are filled with human figures and real and fantastic animals. Crews hoist sails, shift cargoes and hold parasols above important passengers. That these are scenes of princely travel is reinforced by the presence of gamelan orchestras, impressive elephants and horses, and the costume of the retinue and the royal couple, sometimes standing together in an elaborate pavilion. Their voluminous androgynous court dress, *dodot*, today associated largely with the palaces of central Java, is clearly indicated by the pronounced bulge of each skirtcloth. Along with the hilt of a ceremonial *keris* sword seen at the waist of many, these are unambiguous signals of noble origins of the travellers. The *wayang*-style depiction of human figures also echoes Javanese court imagery.

These ships are clearly based on functioning vehicles, with many of the structural mechanisms of local marine engineering articulated in a realistic manner: the construction of masts, the setting of sails, the rudders and oars, the tiny tender drawn behind the main vessel, and the series of upper and lower deck activities. Not only are the decks on these vessels clearly stratified — so too is the cosmos surrounding the ship. Each multilayered scene is a cameo of a symbolic and more imaginative universe, with the world of human activity located between the watery netherworld teeming with marine creatures, including mermaids, and an upper realm filled with birds and spirit boats.

Until the demise of these textile traditions was undoubtedly accelerated by the deadly volcanic explosion in 1883 of Krakatoa (located between the coast of Lampung and the island of Java), every family owned the small *tampan* widely used at such ceremonies. However, it was exclusively the aristocracy of Lampung who controlled the larger shipcloth hangings known as *palepai*. Not only are these cloths displayed at the rites of passage of noble individuals, but they also play an additional role in local ceremonies of state. *Palepai* adorned the walls during formal meetings of local chiefs, at communal activities such as the erection of a clan house and, most appropriately, at the elaborate ceremonies that marked the formal elevation of nobles to higher rank. The carved throne on which the nobleman sat during such pomp was also draped in a spectacular *palepai*. While sharing much of the imagery found on the smaller *tampan*, the imagery of the *palepai* is usually marked by the impressive size of the sailing vessel depicted, especially its elaborate curving prows, the symbolic trees of life that flank the ship and the abundant use of turmeric dyes to create an aristocratic gold glow. The additional embellishments of mirrorwork and gold ribbon and thread created an aura of nobility and wealth whenever such *palepai* were displayed.

While the *palepai* were the most prestigious local textiles for the aristocrats of Lampung, the wealth of their province had ensured access to the finest exotic trade cloths. This Sumatran region became a great treasure-house for ancient and impressive textiles of local, Indian and sometimes ambiguous origins. Ironically, while the history of Lampung's locally produced masterpieces is far from clear and the imagery of even the most vivid shipcloths continues to invite a wide range of interpretations, the variety and quantity of Indian fabrics located in the region have greatly enriched and illuminated the study of the textile exchanges between India and Indonesia.

Further readings
Broeze, F (ed.), *Brides of the Sea: Port Cities of Asia from the 16th to 20th Centuries*, University of Hawaii Press, Honolulu, 1989.
Chaudhuri, KN, *Trade and Civilisation in the Indian Ocean*, Cambridge University Press, Cambridge, 1985.
Gittinger, M, 'The Shipcloths of South Sumatra: Function and Design System', *Bijdragen tot de Taal-, Land- en Volkenkunde*, vol. 132, 1976.
Guy, J, *Woven Cargoes: Indian Textiles in the East*, Thames and Hudson, London, 1998.
Holmgren, RJ, & AE Spertus, 'Tampan Pasisir: Pictorial Documents of an Ancient Indonesian Coastal Culture', in Gittinger, M (ed.), *Indonesian Textiles*, Textile Museum, Washington, D.C., 1980.
McPherson, K, *The Indian Ocean: A History of People and the Sea*, Oxford University Press, Delhi, 1993.
Manguin, P, 'Shipshape Societies: Boat Symbolism and Political Systems in Insular Southeast Asia', in Marr, DG, & AC Milner (eds), *Southeast Asia in the 9th to 14th Centuries*, Institute of Southeast Asian Studies, Singapore, 1986.
Maxwell, R, *Textiles of Southeast Asia: Tradition, Trade and Transformation*, revised edition, Periplus, Singapore, 2003.
Reid, A, *Southeast Asia in the Age of Commerce 1550–1680. Vol. 1: The Lands Below the Winds, and Vol. 2: Expansion and Crisis*, Yale University Press, New Haven, 1988 & 1993.
Taylor, PM, & LV Aragon, *Beyond the Java Sea: Art of Indonesia*, National Museum of Natural History, Smithsonian Institution, Washington, D.C., 1991.

(above)
Kalianda district, Lampung, south Sumatra, Indonesia
Ceremonial hanging [*palepai*]   19th century
handspun cotton, gold ribbon, natural dyes;
supplementary weft weave, appliqué
68.0 x 280.5 cm
Purchased with the assistance of James Mollison 1985
1985.610

(below)
Kalianda district, Lampung, south Sumatra, Indonesia
Ceremonial hanging [*palepai*]   19th century
handspun cotton, natural dyes; supplementary weft weave
64.0 x 286.0 cm
Purchased with the assistance of James Mollison 1985
1985.611

Kalianda district, Lampung, south Sumatra, Indonesia
Mat c. 1915
rattan, paint; interlacing
76.0 x 201.0 cm
Acquired through gift and purchase from the Collection of
Robert J. Holmgren and Anita Spertus, New York, 2000
2000.768

Kalianda district, Lampung, south Sumatra, Indonesia
Ceremonial textile [*tampan*]   19th century
handspun cotton, natural dyes; supplementary weft weave
67.0 x 63.0 cm
1981.1103

Kalianda district, Lampung, south Sumatra, Indonesia
Ceremonial textile [*tampan*]   19th century
handspun cotton, natural dyes; supplementary weft weave
83.0 x 86.0 cm
Conserved with the assistance of Harry Raworth
Acquired through gift and purchase from the Collection of
Robert J. Holmgren and Anita Spertus, New York, 2000
2000.752

Pasisir people
Branti district, Lampung, south Sumatra, Indonesia
Ceremonial textile [*tampan*] 19th century
handspun cotton, natural dyes; supplementary weft weave, twining
70.2 x 65.0 cm
1981.1105

Pasisir people
Semangka Bay, Lampung, south Sumatra, Indonesia
Ceremonial textile [*tampan*] 19th century
handspun cotton, gold thread, dyes; supplementary weft weave
83.0 x 72.0 cm
Acquired through gift and purchase from the Collection of
Robert J. Holmgren and Anita Spertus, New York, 2000
2000.764

Pasisir people
Lampung, south Sumatra, Indonesia
Ceremonial textile [*tampan*]   19th century
handspun cotton, natural dyes; supplementary weft weave
75.0 x 68.0 cm
1984.601

Pasisir people
Lampung, south Sumatra, Indonesia
Ceremonial textile [*tampan*] 19th century
handspun cotton, natural dyes; supplementary weft weave
72.0 x 67.0 cm
Acquired through gift and purchase from the Collection of
Robert J. Holmgren and Anita Spertus, New York, 2000
2000.756

Paminggir people
Lampung, south Sumatra, Indonesia
Woman's ceremonial skirt [*tapis*]   19th century
cotton, silk, natural dyes; warp ikat, embroidery
144.0 x 137.5 cm
1981.1124

Paminggir people
Lampung, south Sumatra, Indonesia
Woman's ceremonial skirt [*tapis*] 19th century
silk, cotton; supplementary weft weave, warp ikat, embroidery
123.0 x 120.0 cm
Acquired through gift and purchase from the Collection of
Robert J. Holmgren and Anita Spertus, New York, 2000
2000.759

Paminggir people
Lampung, south Sumatra, Indonesia
Woman's ceremonial skirt [*tapis*] 19th century
cotton, silk, mica pieces, gold thread; embroidery, appliqué,
warp ikat 131.0 x 118.0 cm
Acquired through gift and purchase from the Collection of
Robert J. Holmgren and Anita Spertus, New York, 2000
2000.933

Paminggir people
Lampung, south Sumatra, Indonesia
Woman's ceremonial skirt [*tapis*] 19th century
silk, cotton; supplementary weft weave, warp ikat, embroidery
126.0 x 123.0 cm
Acquired through gift and purchase from the Collection of
Robert J. Holmgren and Anita Spertus, New York, 2000
2000.797

Paminggir people
Muara Dua, south Sumatra, Indonesia
Woman's ceremonial skirt [*tapis*]   19th century
silk, gold thread, mica; supplementary weft weave,
embroidery, appliqué
123.0 x 120.0 cm
Conserved with the assistance of Lady Joyce C. Wilson, Canberra
Acquired through gift and purchase from the Collection of
Robert J. Holmgren and Anita Spertus, New York, 2000
2000.859

Paminggir people
Lampung, south Sumatra, Indonesia
Lidded box for betel nut ingredients 1875–1899
plant fibre, beads; interlacing, beading, matting
14.0 x 22.0 x 18.0 cm
1984.587

Kalianda district, Lampung, south Sumatra, Indonesia
Ceremonial hanging [*palepai*]   19th century
cotton, gold and silver thread, mirror pieces, gold and silver ribbon;
supplementary weft weave, couching, embroidery, appliqué
63.0 x 267.0 cm
Acquired through gift and purchase from the Collection of
Robert J. Holmgren and Anita Spertus, New York, 2000
2000.789

2 MANDALA AND *MAHABHARATA*
The lasting impact of Indian religious and philosophical imagery

The best known and most admired legacies of the earliest interactions between India and the Indonesia archipelago are the great 8th-century monuments of Borobodur and Loro Jonggrang (Prambanan) in central Java. These huge stone edifices are the most conspicuous and famous of the ruins of the many examples of ancient Buddhist and Hindu religious architecture spread across thousands of kilometres of western and central Indonesia. Each decade more stone ruins are uncovered by farmers clearing fields and labourers constructing roads and other public works, leaving archaeologists struggling to protect, excavate and maintain the far-flung sites.

From the middle of the first millennium of the present era, through sea contact with the Indian subcontinent and with neighbouring Southeast Asia, kingdoms and principalities across Sumatra, Java, Kalimantan (Borneo), Sulawesi and, of course, Bali and nearby islands began to embrace the religions and philosophies of India. Both Buddhism and Hinduism were to enjoy centuries of great popularity, especially with the rulers of the Indonesian archipelago. At times both religions flourished in close proximity. The great Mahayana Buddhist stupa of Borobodur dates from the late 8th to the early 9th century, contemporaneous with the Prambanan complex of temples dedicated to the Hindu deity Shiva, only 100 kilometres to the southeast (closer to the modern royal centre of Jogjakarta). Both are situated on the rich plains of central Java where rice cultivation provided for and still supports the large populations and prosperous royal courts needed to erect temples and shrines of such massive dimensions. Hinduism was to prove more popular for the

Javanese rulers, and as the centres of royal power shifted to eastern Java it was Hinduism that was the dominant creed.

Today Hinduism is only fully embraced on the island of Bali, where the majority of its 12 million inhabitants are Hindu. Bali's landscape is dotted with great and small temple complexes, richly embellished with religious imagery drawn largely from Indian prototypes. These Indian motifs are present in the wide range of visual and performing arts practised on the island — painting, sculpture, masks and puppetry, jewellery and, of course, textiles. In particular the centrality of the great Hindu epics, the *Ramayana* and the *Mahabharata*, is pervasive in dance, *wayang* theatre, carved temple reliefs and on cloth and costume for both temple and palace use. More surprising is the continued inspiration that the artists of Java have drawn from these Indian legends. Five hundred years after the fall of the last Javanese Hindu kingdom of Majapahit, in the late 15th or early 16th century, and despite the gradual spread of Islam through the circles of court and realm, *wayang* performances based on the legendary succession struggles of the Pandawa brothers against their Kurawa cousins in the *Mahabharata* still entrance, entertain and educate great sections of the Javanese community, from president to peasant. The continued importance of the Indian epics is also evident in the batik arts of Java.

Across both Java and Bali, the connection between shadow puppetry and the stylisation of figurative iconography is striking. Gods, demons and heroes are all depicted in what has become the distinct and internationally recognised central Indonesian *wayang* mode: heads in profile with elongated facial features, long noses balanced by elaborately detailed hair and headdress, bodies twisted into three-quarter frontal position with both legs fully displayed again in profile, and disproportionately long segmented arms. This flattened *wayang*

(opposite) Balinese people
Bali, Indonesia
Nobleman's ceremonial skirt cloth [*saput songket* or *kampuh songket*]
(detail) 19th century
silk, gold and silver thread, natural dyes; supplementary weft weave
110.0 x 157.0 cm 1989.401

style clearly differentiates the Hindu arts of Bali from any of the sculptural styles of the Indian subcontinent, today and in the past. Figures on temple reliefs and textiles, in pigment and on paper are invariably depicted in the *wayang* manner in ceremonial art. That Balinese and Javanese artisans alike share these artistic conventions is deeply rooted in the Hindu past. Later east-Javanese Hindu architecture shared much in common with the architecture of modern Bali, including the *wayang*-style depictions on the bas-reliefs on the stone base of temples, remnants of the golden age of the greater Majapahit empire. With time, and arguably with the dominance of Islam in Java, many of the features of the two-dimensional shadow puppet form (*wayang purwa* or *wayang kulit*), such as the exaggerated segmented arms, have become more characteristic.

Throughout Bali the most overtly Hindu imagery appears on textiles intended as hangings in the cycle of religious rites performed at every major temple complex and minor shrine. The best known examples are Hindu images painted onto sized cotton cloth. Rare examples still survive with the pigments, ecru and Chinese inks applied to that oldest form of Indonesian fabric, beaten bark cloth. These hangings are intended for display on the rear walls and around the eaves of temple pavilions. Their imagery ranges from symbols of the gods to sequences from the great Hindu legends.

Other painted textiles include banners and flags that float at the entrances to temples and shrines. Ideally suited for the elongated triangular flags attached to swaying bamboo poles are the images of Basuki, the *naga* serpent. Basuki literally plays a pivotal role in the greatest creation myths associated with Vishnu in his *avatara* or descent to earth in the form of a tortoise, Kurma. While the sacred Mount Mandara rests pillar-like on the back of the tortoise, the body of the serpent entwines it. Then the primordial struggle begins as the gods and demons perform a tug of war with the serpent's body, churning the milky ocean to produce life. While the butter and milk activity is essentially from temperate pastoral India, the image has had enormous appeal to artists in Bali. Many temples throughout the island rest on stone forms of Kurma the tortoise, while the Basuki serpent is emblazoned on flags and banners and on the doorways and balustrades of the temples themselves.

Ancient ancestral beliefs in reptilian forebears are reinforced by the Indian concept of the *naga* rulers of the watery nether-world. The *naga* serpents appear on all forms of art, and textiles are no exception. Often these are composite images of the eternal tussle between the upper and lower worlds — between giant birds and writhing snakes. The bird in many of these depictions is none other than the Garuda, a figure of Hindu origin that also enjoys enormous popularity in the arts

of Indonesia. While the legendary bird's role as the vehicle on which the Hindu deity Vishnu moves explains his regular display in Balinese arts, the Garuda often appears in the textiles of the island alone or in endless combat with the *naga* snake.

However, it is the great Indian epics — the *Ramayana* and *Mahabharata* — that provide the clearest and most appealing narrative scenes on Indonesian textiles. They offer a huge range of imagery, combining theological and philosophical discourse and moral tales with romance, intrigue, dashing chivalry, great battles and, in the case of Java and Bali, comic relief, and even contemporary social comment.

The *Ramayana* is universally popular in the arts of Bali, appearing on many forms of temple hangings. The narrative offers many popular scenarios for the artist, from the expulsion of the fine young prince Lord Rama from his father's kingdom because of his stepmother's conniving, and his sojourn in the forest with his devoted and beautiful wife Sita (or Sinta) and his loyal brother and inseparable companion Laksmana, to Sita's kidnapping and incarceration by the demon king of Lanka, the multi-armed and multi-headed Ravana. Sita is rescued in a fierce and deadly battle by the brothers and their supporters, the army of the monkey King Sugriwa, led by his great white general Hanuman, who build a giant causeway of boulders between the (Indian) mainland and Lanka. Her rescue is often depicted in religious and court art. In many artistic renditions of the story, however, the final scene, where Sita's virtue in the face of Ravana's advances is tested on a fiery pyre, which Agni the ancient Indian God of Fire (from the same Indo-European root for fire as 'ignite') transforms into a lotus to attest her purity, is the key image that recalls the entire epic for devotees. That Rama is also an *avatara* or incarnation of Vishnu may explain the popularity of the image of the bird messenger, the giant Jatayu, who is fatally wounded trying to save Sita from Ravana's clutches; images of the Garuda and Jatayu often appear to be interchangeable in Indonesian art.

In 20th-century Balinese temple art, scenes from the great Hindu epics are usually painted onto surfaces of cloth or wood. In a set of unusual embroidered hangings from north Bali, all in the *ider-ider* valance form for placement under the eaves of an open pavilion, the images are worked in brilliant silk satin stitch, the garments of the characters highlighted with sequins and metal trimming. In one depicting Sita's ordeal she is the central figure on the fire-lotus with Agni behind, while on either side stretch Rama and Laksmana and their supporters, including the white monkey Hanuman. Many of the followers display unlikely animal heads, including an elephant's, on apian torsos — one of the many examples of the eclectic range of deities and demons, spirits and heroes whose forms incorporate anthropomorphic and animal features in Indonesian art.

In its Indonesian versions, the great epic poem *Mahabharata* offers many more tales of heroism, intrigue, valour and tragedy. While the quarrel between the two sets of cousins for succession to the kingdom of Kuraksetra is the catalyst for all these tales, in Indonesia the already complex interweaving of tales that leads to the Pandawas' ultimate victory over the Kurawas is a background for many uniquely local legends. Of the Pandawa brothers the characters of Arjuna and Bima (Wrekudara) are particularly popular: many Indonesian stories from the *Mahabharata* centre on the romantic exploits of the beautiful warrior Arjuna and the ferocious loyalty of the unrefined giant Bima. Because there are such well-established conventions of portraying the characters of the epics, artists are able to easily depict specific characters — by dress and hairstyle, physique and facial features, weapons and other accoutrements, the creatures that are their mounts and vehicles, and wives and lovers. Thus an unusually large figure with craggy nose, bulbous eyes and stolid physique, yet with the long upswept hair and heavy jewellery of nobility, the distinctive black-and-white check skirtcloth and the long dangerous fingernail thrust forward as his weapon, immediately identifies — on textile or shadow puppet — the figure of Bima. Conversely the delicate slim figure of Arjuna clearly defines his royal heritage, while the simplicity of his dress, and in some cases his long flowing hair, indicates his discipline in ascetic practice. The local viewers, however, immediately associate the figure with extraordinary skills as a warrior and in courting women.

The allusion on textiles, as with other art forms, may also be iconographic: on one nobleman's luminous silk wrap a frieze-like hunting may refer to an episode from the epic poem *Arjuna's Wedding* (*Arjuna Wiwaha*) in which Arjuna and the disguised Hindu god Shiva compete in the shooting of a boar. Unlike the fluid and non-repetitive linear depiction that is readily achieved with Javanese hand-drawn batik, the supplementary floating weft brocade technique usually results in a series of mirror images as the weaver returns to the same sets of pattern sheds throughout the length of the cloth. Embroidery also favours the narrative on a valance where the chariot scene signals that this is the Bharatayudha, the final battle between the Pandawa and Kurawa factions. The clever Krisna, another incarnation of Vishnu, is the charioteer for Arjuna, famously advising him of his duty in the face of human weakness. Following the Indian conventions for depicting the Blue God, Krisna is blue-skinned, his weapon (the *cakra* wheel or discus) an indication that he, too, is an *avatara* of Vishnu.

Another lively set of characters in the uniquely Indonesian versions of the Indian epics provides Javanese and Balinese artists with a popular source of images: the Panakawan, the grotesquely shaped and unkempt servants of the legends' main characters, appear in scenes beside their aristocratic masters and mistresses, injecting comic images of slapstick behaviour. On both islands the most readily recognisable clown is Semar (in Bali, Twalen), a demi-god of rotund proportions. Seated with his Panakawan fellows — Gareng, Petruk and Bagong — in front of Bima or Arjuna as they plot battles or engage in philosophical discourse, or even dropping by parachute into a World War II battle scene in which the Pandawa engage military vehicles flying the Japanese flag, Semar is almost omnipresent in the Indonesian versions of Indian epics.

This continued appropriation of figures and episodes from the great Indian epics to illustrate contemporary events indicates the importance of Indian philosophical and religious imagery and its moral application. It is thus not surprising that left-wing artist Mohamad Hadi (1916–1983) chose Srikandi, the warrior wife of Arjuna, as the symbol of his aspirations for the modern Indonesian woman. As the goddess of the women's movement she appears as an aristocrat in breastcloth, elaborate chignon and jewellery; as a more devout Muslim woman in long-sleeved blouse and headcloth; and as the peasant in striped handspun and protective sunhat. The other design on the reversible *pagi-sore* (day and night) cloth shows a key element of the shadow theatre performance. The *gunungan* or *kekayon*, the mountain-tree form, indicates the passage of time and the change of place in the *wayang* narratives. Here the artist uses a readily recognised symbol of transition, which combines the tree of life of ancestral cultures with the sacred mountain of the Indian cosmos, to express his expectations and hope for a rapidly changing and better future for Indonesian women. In Bali, where the most significant *wayang* puppet performances are performed by priestly puppeteers as exorcistic rites for individuals or communities under threat, the *kekayon* tree-mountain figure is among the most potent symbols.

The identification of Hindu gods and heroes by their dress, weapons and other attributes is, of course, Indian in origin, although in the passage of sea and time to 19th- and 20th-century Indonesia the actual renditions of those legendary figures have been regionalised to a point where they bear little resemblance to Indian models. Moreover, on 20th-century Indonesian textiles many of the figures are enigmatic and evocative rather than readily recognisable: a weft-ikat bowman might allude to Rama or may merely be an attractive image appealing to the weaver. On many *lamak* hangings for shrines, however, the reverse operates. Whether in appliquéd palm-leaf or old Chinese coins strung into shapes, or on the rare surviving supplementary warp cotton *lamak*, the series of stark isosceles triangles will always be recognised in Bali as a symbol of the *cili*, representing the goddess of rice and fertility, Dewi Sri, who is a synthesis of the ancient Indonesian rice maiden and Lakshmi, the Hindu goddess of prosperity. In more elaborate but still distinctive hour-glass form, the goddess is depicted with a radiating sunburst headdress.

Many of the most famous Balinese textiles — the double ikat *geringsing* whose patterns appear simultaneously through the combination of warp and weft resist-dyed threads — also display narrative scenes. Their friezes of dark and shadowy features closely resemble the bas-relief images on Hindu temples, while their *wayang*-style figures appear far less distorted by the passage of time and references to shadow puppet stylisation. The cluster of figures around a central shrine also suggests a more overtly devotional setting. This is reinforced by the arrangement of these cameos around bold star-shaped cosmic diagrams that mirror the stepped profiles and floor plans of the temples of Indian religions.

In both Buddhism and Hinduism the universe is pictured diagrammatically: a visual mantra of symbolic geometric forms — squares, circles and triangles — combine in schematic maps of the cosmos. The alignment of the universe with the four (or eight) directions, guarded by demon kings and associated with particular deities (or Buddhas) and their specific weapons, colours and other attributes, has been visualised in mandala forms by artists across Asia for more than a thousand years. In Indonesia this cosmic universe can appear in figurative form, as identifiable Hindu gods brandishing weapons such as the *cakra* and the *vajra* thunderbolt across an embroidered *ider-ider*. More often it provides an attractive and ancient geometric arrangement that resonates with mandala conventions but for which any Buddhist or Hindu meaning has long been lost. Mats and coverings, for offerings and gifts, from the Lampung region of South Sumatra illustrate this very clearly, although the compass points may now be guarded by butterflies rather than demon kings. With a complex design of circles and octagons within squares, both the form and imagery on one of these embroidered coverings suggest great antiquity: the silk and mirror-work embroidery is on indigo-dyed handspun cotton, backed with the most ancient of fabric, beaten bark-cloth.

The south Sumatran regions are rich in mandala designs, a legacy perhaps of the fact that this was the hinterland of one of the greatest early Buddhist pilgrim sites, the epicentre of the 7th–8th-century Indonesian empire of Srivijaya. It is particularly popular as a design frame on square textiles that form the seats for participants and coverings for food and gifts at ceremonies — in village and court — whose origins stretch back to antiquity. With Islam, the offerings to the gods have been supplanted with gifts for honoured guests. However, like the token square shipcloths (*tampan*), many of these textiles have parallels in today's mainland Southeast Asia where they continue to be used in Buddhist ceremonies. In Sumatra the mandala has been transformed into an appealing motif: pokerwork, shimmering silk and mirrors, and thick layers of bead are divided into segmented multilevel squares or burst into compass roses.

It is not surprising that such cosmic diagrams are most popular in those Indonesian regions, like south Sumatra, where Buddhism and Hinduism were strongest. In both Java and Bali a star motif may be analysed as a cosmic symbol, its four points and centre correlated with the gods and colours of the four directions — Visnu (black), Mahadewa (yellow), Brahma (red) and Iswara (white), with the polychrome centre occupied by Siva. Elsewhere the eight-lobed rosette is identified with another ancient Indic image, the lotus, only rarely appearing on textiles as a realistic floral meander.

There are allusions to temple architecture on Balinese textiles where bold mandala forms appear as major motifs and as devices to divide the textile surface into a number of scenes and segments. The appearance of these on the sacred *geringsing* is often in combination with other motifs from religious architecture — shrines, stupas and gargoyles. The power of the *geringsing*, however, lies as much in its materials and making as in the magnetism of its mandala. It is at its most potent when removed from the simple back-strap loom as a handspun cotton circular cloth; in this form it is a very appropriate gift for the gods. The cutting of its warp releases exorcistic healing powers, after which it serves as an item of costume for religious and communal rites. Such is its residual potency that a fragment removed and burned provides the base for curative balms and medicines. The designs on the more secular and decorative weft ikat and *songket* brocades, which added splendour to palace ceremony, often echo the mandala patterning of the sombre sacred *geringsing* cottons.

In Bali motifs frequently recur in different media. The dramatic architectural device of a mask-like demonic face that protects the entrance to the temples is a recurring motif on textiles. Known across the Hindu-Buddhist world as the *kirtimukha*, it takes myriad forms (and names) in Bali, with a central eye or two bulging eyes, with or without the lower jaw, jagged fangs pointing up or down, face sometimes flanked by claw-like hands. All these can be found on cloths for both temple and palace; where the demonic face dominates a textile, it provides similar protective functions as when it appears above the arch into the temple's inner sanctum. On a set of rare examples of Balinese noblemen's over-wraps, the motif appears as a complete demon's head, with dripping tongue and a halo of hair. Appearing as a symbol of the elements, it is also a reminder of the enduring devotion to the more ancient Vedic gods of India associated with the seasons and weather, such as Surya the sun god, Indra god of storms, Varuna god of rains and Agni god of fire, and to the goddess of fertility in agricultural Bali.

Like its architectural counterpart, on fabric the demonic mask also appears in the company of writhing serpents and *wayang*-style figures from the Hindu epics. The arrangement of scenes from the epics around shrine-like structures and within split gateways brings the temple into focus and suggests that, even when created with the most luxurious and costly materials, these are sacred images with exorcistic powers. The arrangement of the demonic heads in the borders of the cloths, replacing the ubiquitous jagged triangles, provides a protective guard for the central design and for the wearer of the garment. On some old Lombok cloths, remnants of rites no longer performed by that island's syncretic Islamic communities are evident in the guardian motifs at the borders, where the paraphernalia of Hindu-Buddhist ritual — candelabras, golden wishing trees and architectural forms — still appear.

Perhaps the starkest instance of the use of textiles for protection in Hindu Bali are the *tumbal rajah*, often placed, like the *kirtimukha*, above doorways. The *tumbal rajah*, however, are transitory textiles to be destroyed by the elements as they perform their talismanic function. Seen at the entrance to family compounds and to communal venues, many are rough inscriptions and cartoon-like drawings on white cotton. They harness the demonic side of the supernatural world, using black magic to outwit the dangerous and demonic forces that threaten individuals and groups.

Bali and Java are dotted with sacred banyan trees, ancient temples and the presence of shrines in domestic settings and mountain retreats. This landscape has provided imagery for the rulers of Java, whose realms are both spiritual and temporal. A number of key textile designs, especially in Java where the importance of asceticism and mysticism has transcended different religious orientations, focus on the sacred spirited landscape, imbued with supernatural forces. The often schematic designs usually feature chevron patterns of mountains scattered with pavilions and shrines amid impressions of foliage, especially the distinctive aerial roots of the sacred banyan. The allusions to Mount Meru, the dwelling place of the gods in Indian religions, is clear and the popularity of retreats to holy places on the peaks of mountainous Java — for rulers, heroes and sages — continues to the present day.

Usually hand-drawn in batik, a very flexible medium for these very fluid scenes, some landscape renditions include a menagerie of real animals. The legendary *naga* serpent is most commonly imbedded in the landscape, slipping through ponds below shrines or in interlocked pairs throughout. Its nemesis, the giant Garuda, symbol of the ruler of the realm, is also a recurring motif in stylised form as a single wing or as pairs of wings scattered throughout and as a bold heraldic emblem in the corners of a royal wrap. On rare examples of royal textiles the key elements of the landscape may be highlighted in gold leaf.

Textiles in the Indonesian realms under the influence of Buddhism and Hinduism, today and in the distant past, continue to display motifs and designs drawn from Indian religious and cosmological imagery. This may be the faint imprint of the mandala, or the bold narrative of the *Mahabharata*. Yet, even where Hinduism flourishes in Bali, the forms of the textiles, the techniques by which they are created, and the imagery they exploit share much in common with ancestral communities across the spread of Indonesia. In particular the historical development of the quintessentially Indonesian flat *wayang* figuration distances even the most Indian of images stylistically from their renditions at the point of origin in India over a thousand years ago.

Further readings
Fontein, J, *The Sculpture of Indonesia*, Harry N Abrams, New York, 1990.
Forge, A, *Balinese Traditional Paintings*, Australian Museum, Sydney, 1978.
Hauser-Schäublin, B, Nabholz-Kartaschoff, M, & U Ramseyer, *Balinese Textiles*, British Museum Press, London, 1991.
Jessup, HI, *Court Arts of Indonesia*, Harry N Abrams, New York, 1990.
Maxwell, R, 'The Figurative Textiles of Bali', in Menzies, J (ed.), *Donald Friend's Bali*, Art Gallery of New South Wales, Sydney 1990.
Miksic, J, *Borobodur: Golden Tales of the Buddhas*, Periplus, Singapore, 1990.
Ramseyer, U, *The Art and Culture of Bali*, Oxford University Press, Oxford, 1977.
Van Hout, IC (ed.), *Batik — Drawn in Wax: 200 Years of Batik Art from Indonesia in the Tropenmuseum Collection*, Koninklijk Instituut, Amsterdam, 2001.
Veldhuisen-Djajasoebrata, A, *Weaving of Power and Might: The Glory of Java*, Museum voor Volkenkunde, Rotterdam, 1988.
Vickers, A, 'From Bali to Lampung by Way of the Pasisir', *Archipel*, vol. 45, 1993.

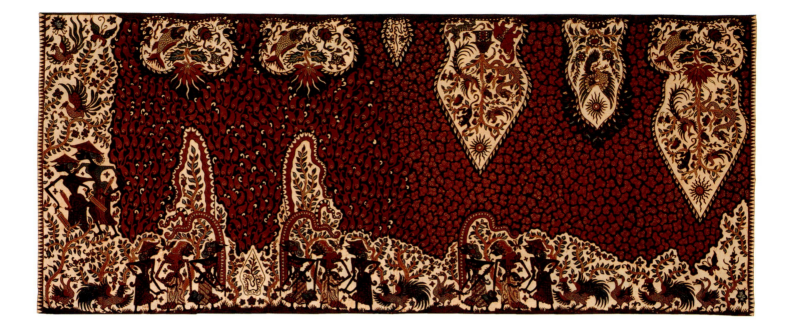

(above) HADI, Mohamad [1916–1983]
Surakarta, Java, Indonesia
Srikandi as goddess of the Indonesian Women's Movement [*Srikandi Gerwani*] 1964
cotton, natural dyes; hand-drawn batik
106.0 x 251.5 cm
Purchased with Gallery Shop Funds 1984
1984.3065

(below) Javanese people
Jogjakarta, Java, Indonesia
Skirt cloth [*kain panjang*] c. 1942
cotton, natural dyes; hand-drawn batik
106.0 x 240.0 cm
Purchased with Gallery Shop Funds 1984
1984.3110

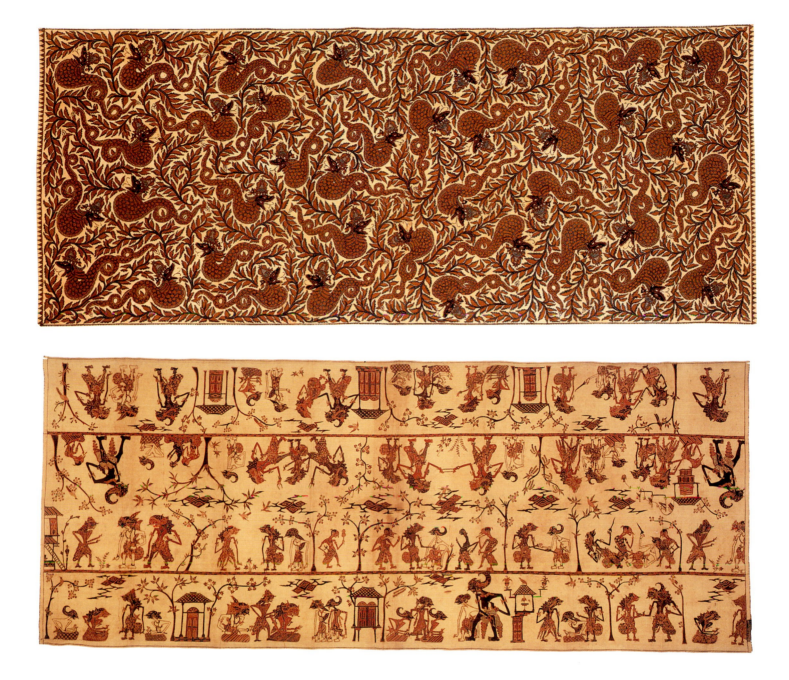

(above) HARDJONAGORO, Kangjeng Raden Tumenggung [born 1931]
Surakarta, Java, Indonesia
Skirt cloth [*kain panjang*]   1960–1969
cotton, natural dyes; hand-drawn batik
105.5 x 254.0 cm
Purchased with Gallery Shop Funds 1984
1984.3051

(below) Cirebon, Java, Indonesia
Hanging or banner depicting scenes from the *Mahabharata*   1875–1899
cotton, natural dyes; hand-drawn batik
106.5 x 260.0 cm
Purchased with Gallery Shop Funds 1984
1984.3101

(above) Balinese people
Buleleng district, Bali, Indonesia
Valance for a temple or royal pavilion [*ider-ider*]   1875–1899
cotton, silk, dyes, sequins, tinsel; embroidery, appliqué
42.5 x 278.0 cm
Gift of Michael and Mary Abbott 1987
1987.1084

(below) Balinese people
North Bali, Indonesia
Valance for a temple or pavilion [*ider-ider*]   19th century
silk, cotton, dyes, tinsel, sequins; embroidery, appliqué
Conserved with the assistance of Ella Keough
43.5 x 264.0 cm
1985.1740

Balinese people
North Bali, Indonesia
Valance for a temple or pavilion [*ider-ider*] 1875–1899
silk, dyes, cotton, gold thread, tinsel, sequins, glass beads;
appliqué, embroidery, couching
40.0 x 337.0 cm
Conserved with the assistance of the Quilt Study Group of Australia, Canberra Branch
Gift of Michael and Mary Abbott 1988
1988.1579

Balinese people
Bali, Indonesia
Nobleman's ceremonial textile [*kampuh songket* or *saput songke*t]   19th century
silk, gold and silver thread, natural dyes; supplementary weft weave
108.5 x 105.0 cm
Gift of Michael and Mary Abbott 1988
1988.1578

Balinese people
Bali, Indonesia
Nobleman's ceremonial skirt wrap [*kampuh songket* or *saput songket*]   19th century
silk, gold thread, dyes; supplementary weft weave
109.5 x 157.0 cm
1989.407

(opposite) Javanese people
Jogjakarta, Java, Indonesia
Royal ceremonial skirt cloth [*dodot pinarada mas*]
1900–1925
cotton, silk, natural dyes, gold leaf;
hand-drawn batik, gold-leaf gluework, appliqué
379.0 x 210.5 cm
1984.3165

(far left) Sasak people
Lombok, Indonesia
Ceremonial textile [*pesujutan*] 19th century
cotton, natural dyes; supplementary weft weave
215.5 x 55.0 cm
Gift of Michael and Mary Abbott 1990
1990.1278

(left) Balinese people
Kesiman, Badung district, Bali, Indonesia
Shrine hanging [*lamak*] late 19th – early 20th
century
handspun cotton, natural dyes, mirror, brass, sequins,
gold ribbon;
supplementary warp weave, appliqué, embroidery
163.0 x 42.0 cm
1989.496

Balinese people
Bali, Indonesia
Exorcistic cloth [*tumbal rajah*]   1900–1925
cotton, pigments, ink; painting, writing
88.0 x 148.0 cm
1980.1635

Cirebon, Java, Indonesia
Skirt cloth [*kain panjang*]   mid 20th century
cotton, dyes; hand-drawn batik
106.0 x 255.0 cm
1984.3100

To Bada or To Kaili people
Bada or Kulawi district, Sulawesi, Indonesia
Man's head cloth [*siga*] c. 1900
bark cloth, pigments; painting
85.0 x 85.0 cm
Acquired through gift and purchase from the Collection of
Robert J. Holmgren and Anita Spertus, New York, 2000
2000.707

To Bada or To Kaili people
Bada or Kulawi district, Sulawesi, Indonesia
Man's head cloth [*siga*] c. 1900
bark cloth, pigments; painting
99.0 x 98.0 cm
Acquired through gift and purchase from the Collection of
Robert J. Holmgren and Anita Spertus, New York, 2000
2000.713

Paminggir people
Lampung, south Sumatra, Indonesia
Ceremonial mat [*lampit*]   1875–1900
rattan, cotton; twining, burnt pokerwork
90.0 x 100 cm
1984.602

Paminggir people
Lampung, south Sumatra, Indonesia
Nobleman's mat of honour [*lampit*]   19th century
rattan, cotton; twining, burnt pokerwork
81.0 x 92.0 cm
Acquired through gift and purchase from the Collection of
Robert J. Holmgren and Anita Spertus, New York, 2000
2000.829

Lampung, south Sumatra, Indonesia
Ceremonial cover for food or gifts   19th century
cotton, gold thread, silver thread, sequins, silk, mirror pieces;
embroidery, appliqué, couching
68.0 x 70.0 cm
Acquired through gift and purchase from the Collection of
Robert J. Holmgren and Anita Spertus, New York, 2000
2000.839

Abung people
Kota Bumi district, south Sumatra, Indonesia
Ceremonial cloth c. 1900
bark cloth, cotton, silk, dyes, gold thread, mirror pieces;
embroidery, couching, appliqué
67.0 x 67.5 cm
1980.1629

Paminggir people
Lampung, south Sumatra, Indonesia
Ceremonial covering [*tampan maju*]   19th century
rattan, cotton, beads, shells; appliqué, beading
59.0 x 71.0 cm
Acquired through gift and purchase from the Collection of
Robert J. Holmgren and Anita Spertus, New York, 2000
2000.761

Paminggir people
Lampung, south Sumatra, Indonesia
Ceremonial mat [*tampan maju*; *selesil*]   19th century
cotton, rattan, beads, shells; interlacing, appliqué
67.0 x 118.0 cm
1983.3689

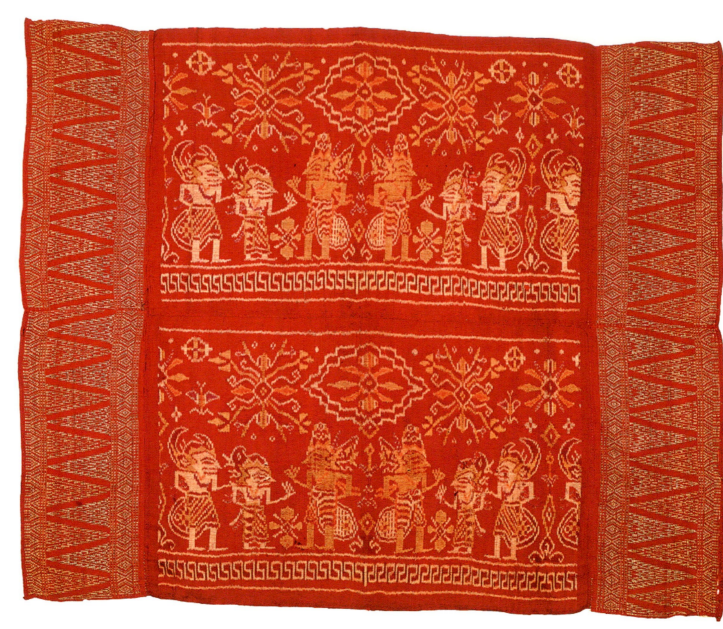

Balinese people
Bali, Indonesia
Man's ceremonial wrap [*saput endek* or *kampuh endek*]   early 20th century
silk, gold thread, dyes; supplementary weft weave, weft ikat
109.0 x 133.0 cm
1989.413

(above) Balinese people
Bali, Indonesia
Man's ceremonial wrap [*saput songket* or *kampuh songket*]   1900–1925 (detail)
silk, gold thread, dyes; supplementary weft weave
119.5 x 133.0 cm
1989.408

(below) Balinese people
Bali, Indonesia
Shoulder or breast cloth [*selendang* or *kamben*]   1900–1925
silk, natural dyes; weft ikat
221.0 x 43.0 cm
1989.417

Balinese people
Bali, Indonesia
Man's ceremonial wrap [*saput songket* or *kampuh songket*]   1900–1925
silk, gold thread, dyes; supplementary weft weave
98.0 x 133.0 cm
1989.409

Balinese people
Bali, Indonesia
Nobleman's ceremonial wrap [*saput endek* or *kampuh endek*]   1900–1925
silk, gold thread, dyes; supplementary weft weave, weft ikat
106.0 x 125.0 cm
1989.414

(above) Balinese people
Bali, Indonesia
Nobleman's ceremonial wrap [*saput songket* or *kampuh songket*]   early 20th century
silk, gold thread, dyes; supplementary weft weave, weft ikat
136.0 x 107.6 cm
1989.404

(opposite) Balinese people
Bali, Indonesia
Man's ceremonial wrap [*saput songket* or *kampuh songket*]   19th century
silk, gold thread, dyes; supplementary weft weave
93.5 x 143.5 cm
1989.398

Balinese people
Bali, Indonesia
Nobleman's ceremonial skirt cloth [*saput songket* or *kampuh songket*]   19th century
silk, gold and silver thread, natural dyes; supplementary weft weave
110.0 x 157.0 cm
1989.401

Balinese people
Bali, Indonesia
Banner [*lontek*]   c. 1930
cotton, pigments; painting
86.6 x 363.4 cm
Gift of Michael and Mary Abbo[...]
1989.1321

Paminggir people
Lampung, south Sumatra, Indonesia
Ceremonial textile [*tampan*]   19th–20th century
cotton, natural dyes; supplementary weft weave
73.0 x 73.0 cm
1981.1104

Paminggir people
Lampung, south Sumatra, Indonesia
Ceremonial textile [*tampan*] 19th century
cotton, natural dyes; supplementary weft weave
58.0 x 69.0 cm
Acquired through gift and purchase from the Collection of
Robert J. Holmgren and Anita Spertus, New York, 2000
2000.773

Paminggir people
Lampung, south Sumatra, Indonesia
Ceremonial textile [*tampan*]   19th century
cotton, natural dyes; supplementary weft weave
66.0 x 67.0 cm
Acquired through gift and purchase from the Collection of
Robert J. Holmgren and Anita Spertus, New York, 2000
2000.805

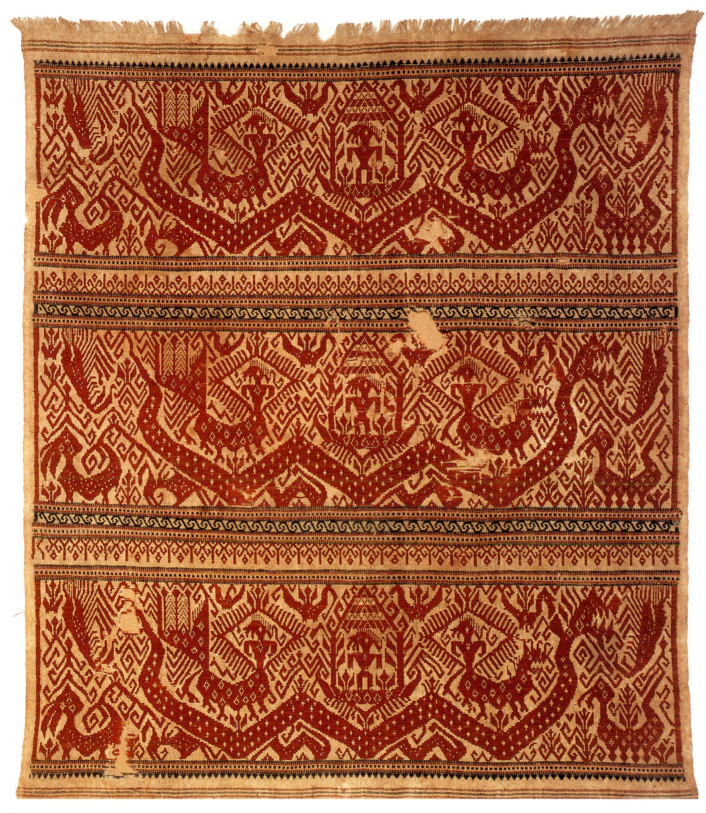

Paminggir people
Lampung, south Sumatra, Indonesia
Ceremonial textile [*tampan*] 19th century
cotton, natural dyes; supplementary weft weave
78.0 x 66.0 cm
1984.257

(above) Balinese people
Tenganan, Bali, Indonesia
Sacred textile [*geringsing wayang*]   19th century
cotton, dyes; double ikat
47.0 x 203.0 cm
Acquired through gift and purchase from the Collection of
Robert J. Holmgren and Anita Spertus, New York, 2000
2000.750

(below) Balinese people
Tenganan, Bali, Indonesia
Sacred textile [*geringsing wayang kebo*]   late 19th century
cotton, dyes, gold thread; double ikat, embroidery
54.0 x 212.0 cm
1982.2308

Balinese people
Bali, Indonesia
Nobleman's ceremonial wrap [*saput endek* or *kampuh endek*]
early 20th century
silk, natural dyes; weft ikat
115.0 x 137.0 cm
1984.1539

Balinese people
Bali, Indonesia
Nobleman's ceremonial wrap [*saput endek* or *kampuh endek*]   19th century
silk, gold thread, dyes; supplementary weft weave, weft ikat
112.0 x 166.0 cm
1989.420

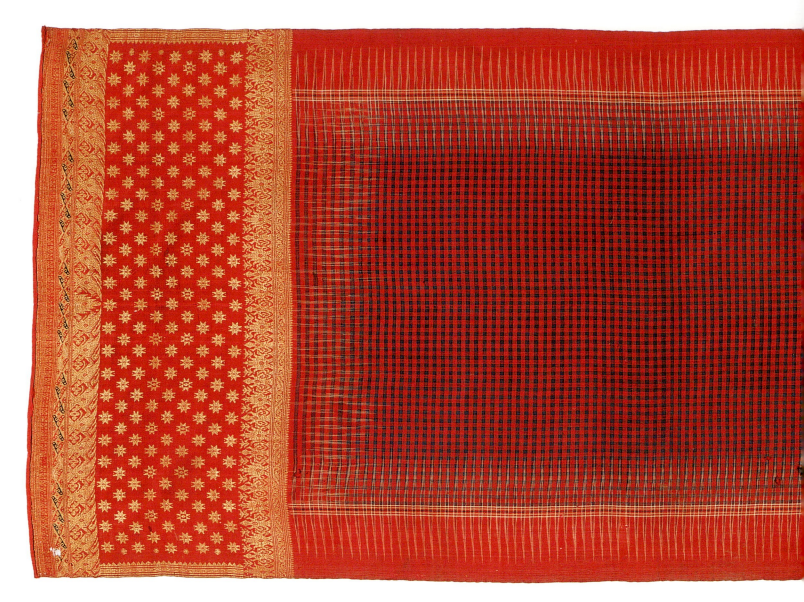

Minangkabau people
Sijunjung, west Sumatra, Indonesia
Ceremonial shoulder cloth [*selendang*]　19th century
silk, gold thread, dyes; weft and warp ikat, supplementary weft weave
206.0 x 77.0 cm
Acquired through gift and purchase from the Collection of
Robert J. Holmgren and Anita Spertus, New York, 2000
2000.914

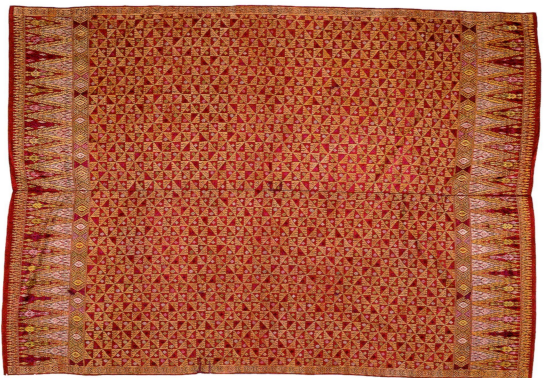

Javanese people
Jogjakarta, Java, Indonesia
Baby-carrier [*kain selendang; kain gedongan*]   early 20th century
cotton, natural dyes; hand-drawn batik
278.0 x 75.0 cm
Conserved with the assistance of the Textile Focus Group Members and T.A.A.S.A. (Vic)
1987.344

(opposite above) Balinese people
Singaraja, Bali, Indonesia
Nobleman's ceremonial wrap [*saput songket* or *kampuh songket*]   19th century
silk, gold thread, silver thread, cotton; supplementary weft weave, braid weave
124.0 x 175.0 cm
Acquired through gift and purchase from the Collection of
Robert J. Holmgren and Anita Spertus, New York, 2000
2000.844

(opposite below) Balinese people
Bali, Indonesia
Nobleman's ceremonial wrap [*saput songket* or *kampuh songket*]
early 20th century
silk, gold thread, dyes; supplementary weft weave
139.2 x 199.8 cm
1989.403

3 G O L D , G L O R Y A N D G L A M O U R
Textiles in the Indonesian royal courts

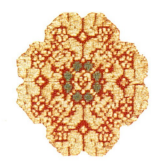

From the first centuries AD, the increasing contacts with India encouraged the adoption of Indian religious and political concepts throughout Southeast Asia. These ideas supported and enhanced the growing consolidations of populations into forming local states under dynastic rule. In Indonesia these kingdoms were largely established in the western and central islands on the central lowland plains and coastal regions. The power of the rulers of these newly forming states was based both on feudal agricultural systems and, increasingly over the next millennium, on control of the burgeoning regional and international trade. As the latter became a source of wealth and influence, small principalities and city-states continued to mushroom throughout coastal and riverine Indonesia. Many conceived of or fashioned themselves as the descendants of legendary early empires.

As local dynastic rule was established over these emerging centres in the first millennium AD, Indian religions had enormous appeal. A powerful and successful prince was perceived as a universal monarch and a just ruler, only a step away from achieving enlightenment in the cycle of rebirths. His or her patronage of great architectural edifices was not only a sign of piety and a means of gaining merit in the supernatural sphere but a symbol of prestige in the earthly realm. Palaces resembled the heavenly abodes of the gods, with troupes of musicians and dancers, tournaments in spacious grounds, yogic retreats in spirited landscapes, feasts in stately pavilions and barges on ornamental pools. The monarch paraded through the realm in elaborate palanquins,

on noble elephants and in horse-drawn carriages, accompanied by impressive processions of courtiers, with palace guards in train. Court ritual bristled with symbols of the god-king — parasols of rank, raised lotus thrones, auspicious geometry, magic weapons, wishing trees (or the tree of life), offerings in the forms of candelabra and sacred mountains, performances of the great Indian epics, and images of real and mythical creatures embodying the noble or ferocious attributes of Garuda birds, lions, elephants and serpents. Royal genealogies, dynastic histories and epic poems constituted the literature of the courts, which embraced Indian Sanskrit scripts and palm-leaf manuscripts. Many of the appropriate terms associated with courtly and religious ceremonies were adopted from India, the most obvious being the generic terms for rulers throughout Indonesia — *raja* and *maharaja*.

While the religious affiliation of the royal courts of Java shifted from Hinduism to Islam from the middle of the second millennium AD, the ceremonial life of the palace and realm continued to follow established patterns. Moreover, throughout the littoral regions of Sumatra, Borneo and Sulawesi, the smaller kingdoms that controlled the strategic crossroads, safe harbours and estuaries of large rivers admired and consciously emulated the Javanese model of statecraft. In those kingdoms similar Indian-inspired symbols of rank and power were widely adopted. Even the diminishing power and wealth of regional monarchies in the face of European intervention and their ultimate subjugation to the Dutch East Indies colonial government failed to extinguish courtly pageant: the ancient royal symbols might ossify, but they persisted such that many of the late 19th-century symbols of the courts of north and central Java mirrored those of Hindu Bali. And while the Malay sultanates transcribed their dynastic histories and legends in Arabic script, the Javanese courts continued to favour the Indian scripts of earlier golden eras.

(opposite) Acehnese people
Aceh, north Sumatra, Indonesia
Ceremonial hanging [*bi*] early 20th century (detail)
cotton, wool, silk, gold thread, sequins, glass beads, mica;
appliqué, lace, couching, embroidery
64.0 x 208 cm
1984.1986

The fluorescence of art associated with the Indianised kingdoms of Indonesia is well documented, at least with regards to stone and metal. However, the tropical conditions of the region have not favoured the survival of the textiles or wooden loom apparatus from those early historical times. Fragments of textile history, however, can be discovered in the sculptures and bas-relief scenes of the classical periods and in records of early travellers and ambassadors to the courts of Southeast Asia.

Everywhere, past and present, in Asia and in Europe, gold evokes similar responses and signals clear messages: the owner controls great wealth and power, and he or she possesses objects of enormous value, created by the most talented artisans. Indonesia has been no exception. Early Sanskrit versions of the *Ramayana* allude to Sumatra and Java as Lands of Gold and the Island of Gold and Silver, as did Roman texts from the first century of the present era. The rulers of Indonesia's great empires and tiny principalities, particularly those established in regions closest to India and the trade routes, were renowned for their conspicuous display of objects made of gold, especially elaborate jewellery, other items of regalia and the gold-encrusted garments that were the stuff of legends. Even the early European travellers and ambassadors to the courts of the region were impressed by the gold 'embroidered' costume of the rulers, although they were somewhat askance at the exposed upper bodies of king and courtiers.

The Indonesian princes who received the European delegations were certainly Islamic. Their court protocols and dress, however, were an amalgam of customs and ceremonies that dated back to Hindu and Buddhist times. The feudal kingdoms of Java, like those of Angkor-period Cambodia, depended on a hierarchical system of serfs and slaves to build the great stone edifices that have survived to today. While the caste systems of India never developed to the same strengths in Indonesia, the distinction between ruler and subject was always very well-articulated and visualised in many ways, none less so than differences in the size and décor of the domicile and of dress.

One of the most important and long-lasting ways of symbolising the wealth and power of the court has been through sumptuous dress. The history of high status textiles, especially those created from silk and gold, has been intimately tied to the rise of royal court centres throughout the Indonesian region from as early as the first millennium AD. In historical times experts in gold smithing and textile weaving gravitated to the royal capitals, often synonymous with the port centres in the Malay world. The control of produce and trade — international, inter-island and internally between hinterland and the port centres — through taxes and tribute not only provided the wealth to support royal luxury and extravagance of dress and furnishings, but also guaranteed access to the materials from which the most valuable cloth was created.

The courts operated as conduits for objects and ideas, and among the products of trade and tribute were fine textiles and their major components, silk and gold thread. While Indonesia was a major source of gold and local sericulture did develop in parts of the archipelago, the threads from which the gold cloth was woven were largely imported.

The conjunction of these luxurious and exotic fibres with the development of a hierarchical social structure of centralised dynastic rule, manifest in finely regulated systems of rank based on the patronage of the omnipotent ruler, resulted in a very different textile complex from that based on ancestral and animist beliefs and within small-scale clan-based domains. Throughout Indonesia the cultural distinctions that developed between the inner states and the wider outer region, between centre and periphery, between the lowlands and the hinterlands, appear to have been mirrored within each kingdom, in the relationships between the court and the village. These dichotomies were reflected in material ways, including the textile arts. Silk textiles, ornamented with gold, became the focus of a very different set of symbolic meanings from those made from the ancient vegetable fibres. Yet, since the distinctions between court and village were based on sumptuary laws that also governed types of clothing and designs and proscribed the use of luxury fabrics for anyone outside the aristocratic elite, both types of textiles necessarily coexisted.

There are numerous techniques used by Indonesian artists to decorate cloth with gold for aristocratic use: gold thread was interwoven into brocades, gold leaf and gold dust were adhered to the surface of fabrics, and gold thread and coloured silks were stitched into embroideries. While embroidery was a popular means of creating elaborate furnishings for ceremonies of state, it was less widely used for garments. Gold could not only be incorporated into fabric in the weaving, but it was able to be added to luxury fabric of many types. In many cases the gold leaf emulates the pattern woven into brocades; in other instances it gilded the liner designs of a batik base cloth. The most time-consuming yet most enduring textiles were the gold and silk brocades, widely known throughout Indonesia as *songket*. Gold-wrapped thread, sometimes with additional silver and silk, floats across a colourful woven silk background. In past centuries the rich *songket* brocading was often combined with complex weft ikat patterning, achieved by tie-dyeing the weft threads into multicoloured designs before weaving them into a monochrome silk warp. The result was the fabulous *kain songket limar* for which the weavers of many of the archipelago's court centres were renowned.

Perhaps surprisingly the techniques by which the silk and gold *songket* textiles were created in Indonesia did not follow Indian (or Chinese) loom technology. One concession appears to have been the adoption of the spinning wheel for thread production in regions historically influenced by India: throughout the archipelago the instrument is known by variations of the term *jantra*, derived from the Sanskrit term for wheel, *cakra*. Arguably the reason for the conservative nature of textile technology has been the fact that throughout Indonesia the production of fine textiles, whether for courtly use or for ancestral rites, remained firmly in the hands of women. The Indian distinction between the roles of women and men in the creation of textiles for domestic and commercial use, and between village and court was not adopted in the Indonesian archipelago until very modern times. In contrast to the male weavers and embroiderers in the royal Mughal workshops or in the many centres where men have historically dominated the weaving and block-printing of textiles for temple use and international trade, in both the courts and villages of Indonesia textiles are exclusively a female art.

However, between court and village, and between Indianised Indonesia and the staunchly ancestral domains of the mountainous uplands and the more remote islands, quite fundamental shifts occurred in the meaning and function of textiles. Silk and gold textiles in the Indic courts were not just the preferred fabric for state ceremonials: they provided a means of visualising the complex status systems that supported court ritual. Thus the formal relationship of subjects to the ruler, his recognition and patronage, and the resulting honours and office were reflected in the pomp and ceremony and especially in the garments worn on occasions of state ritual.

Most significant for the symbolic meaning of textiles was the fact that the ancient distinctions of gender and age were supplanted by differentiations in rank and social status. Textiles no longer identified family or clan origins, marital status or the maturity of cultural knowledge and age. Most fundamentally, however, in the sphere of the Indonesian court the textiles ceased to indicate gender differences. The silk and gold textiles of the courts instead signified differences in social hierarchy and rank, irrespective of the gender of the wearer. Whether flat rectangular fabrics of fixed proportions and set design structure or lengths stitched into cylindrical skirtcloths (the *sarong* form), the expensive items could be worn by male or female, provided that they suitably reflected the status of the aristocratic wearer. While subtle gender differences continued to be incorporated — for instance, cloths being wrapped to left or right depending on the gender of the wearer — the main symbolic message was asexual, as silk textiles were instead imbued with and understood as symbols of high status.

The designs displayed on these silk and gold textiles demonstrate many international influences. While the wraps of Balinese noblemen display vignettes from the Hindu epics, Malay brocades are filled with schematic patterns and floral nuances more attune with the much admired decorative arts of Mughal India. Framed within decorative border meanders and enclosed at each end by elaborate designs, often incorporating triangular patterns, the field patterns are a reflection of the cosmopolitan sources available for designers of luxury textiles and the multicultural flavour of the Indonesian city states. The elaborate end designs are a decorative feature when the long rectangular textile is wrapped around the lower torso, falling in ornamental folds down the front of the body. This is the most prominent garment to be observed on the sculpture of classical Hindu and Buddhist Indonesia. The garments of, and the way they are worn by, male and female deities, and also royal couples, are indistinguishable and often precisely matching in design and patterns.

Over time, especially in the coastal Islamic courts, the design structure of the textiles was modified: the end designs were consolidated into a single imposing head panel of confronting triangles, and a continuous field was formed by stitching the flat fabric into a cylindrical skirtcloth, the *sarong*. The decorative panel is variously worn as the rear or gathered, like the earlier forms, into decorative front folds. In each instance, however, it is the content, intricacy and elaboration of the designs and the rare, exotic qualities imbued with economic and social value epitomised by sumptuous raw materials that are the essential features of the silk and gold-brocade textiles. A further feature of the production of silk and gold textiles was the relationship between the maker and the wearer. While the weaving of exquisite textiles continued to be solely the domain of women, the taboos associated with the distinct yet complementary realms of male and female activities appear to have diminished. Certain designs are even attributed to male courtiers, executed by their female companions. In fact the establishment of groups of skilled artisans within the court compounds or immediate vicinity of the palace ensured the court supplies of luxury fabric. While princesses continued to create beautiful cloth, it was no longer to meet the recurring demands of ancestral beliefs and ritual exchange.

The function of ancient vegetable fibre textiles in minutely flagging the wearer's regional and linguistic associations was supplanted in the courts by an international textile form that transcended the borders of principalities and echoed the trans-Indonesian penchant for imported luxury fabrics. Delicate distinctions in social rank, however, were variously encoded in textiles, although this sometimes varied from one kingdom to the next. Some textile hierarchies depended on the number, size and content of the triangular bands across the ends of the fabric. The length of the skirtcloth and concomitantly the amount of leg or trouser visible could also indicate differentiations in rank for male courtiers, the height of the hem of the skirtcloth often reflecting the eminence of the wearer. Although the dominant background of the silk fabrics across most of Indonesia is a rich lac red, different colours were also important within the hierarchical status system of certain courts. Across Indonesia it is yellow, often a fugitive dye from turmeric-related tubers, that is generally reserved for the ruler and his immediate family, especially his heirs. Gifts were wrapped in golden yellow silks, and yellow garments, particularly pants and jackets, were created for the ruler's exclusive wear. In areas such as Lampung in southern Sumatra where cotton textiles remained the basis for the gold and silk embroideries of aristocratic families, turmeric was often the dominant colour, its warm golden hues a foil for the crisp bands of needlework. While yellow is rarely found on the more democratic *tampan*, many of the finest *palepai* shipcloths that were the reserve of the Lampung nobility are generously infused with turmeric yellow, with additional highlights of mirrors, sequins and gold ribbon to attest the importance of the ruler at whose ceremonies of state the hanging was displayed.

Across the Indonesian region, loose conjunctions of textile meanings, in association with certain basic materials and techniques, can be identified. Major differentiations can be made between, for example, symbolic associations surrounding beaten bark cloth, batik and categories of woven fabric. The weaving and wearing of the *songket* cloth-of-gold is no exception. These textiles woven from silk and metallic thread may be distinguished from those woven from vegetable fibres such as palm-leaf, reed, bast and, increasingly in recent centuries, cotton. On one level this distinction may be viewed in terms of expense: vegetable fibres, including handspun cotton, are readily available locally, while silk and gold thread have long been exotic and valuable imported commodities acquired through trade. These textile complexes are in fact a visual manifestation of very basic underlying dichotomies discussed earlier — between centre and periphery, between uplands and lowlands, between mountain and sea, and between the world of ancestral Indonesia and one redolent with Indian symbols of royalty and state.

Throughout Indonesia both the silk and the vegetable fibre fabrics are woven on an archaic form of loom, the back-tension or back-strap loom, which was arguably part of the technology of the region's early immigrants. It is still widely used in Indonesia. In the upland and outer island regions of the archipelago it is used to weave vegetable fibres, today almost invariably cotton. On this simple device the cotton threads that will form the warp are wrapped around breast beam and warp beam in a continuous circulating warp; on completion of the weaving, the fabric is removed from the loom with the circular warp uncut. In the court centres of Indonesia, especially the western and central islands, a modified form of the same back-tension loom, incorporating a reed or comb, is used to weave silk and metallic thread.

The orientation of the patterning on the vegetable fibre textiles formed with circulating warps is warp oriented and warp faced, usually achieved with warp ikat and supplementary warp techniques. In contrast the silk and gold brocades are usually weft faced and decorated with supplementary weft and weft ikat techniques. However, it is the symbolic meaning attached to the circular warps that is fundamental to understanding the enduring importance of vegetable fibre fabrics in the region and the very different symbolic meaning of the silk and gold brocades. In ancestral rites the potency of the textile is generally encapsulated in its circular form. It may require a ritual cutting of the warp to generate the textile's sacred potency or it may only be textiles with intact circulating warps that have currency in the elaborate encoded exchanges of male and female goods that accompany marriage settlements and are conspicuously present at all rites of passage, from birth to death. Thus the sacred power of a textile may be activated or dissipated through the cutting of the warp. In rare instances a completely woven, unseamed cylindrical cloth may be produced, imbued with ritual power. In village Bali, cotton textiles with circulating warps vary from simple loosely woven warp-striped sashes to the intricate double ikat *geringsing*; in each case the textiles are seen to contain sacred energy able to be harnessed by the individual or community in ceremonies of exorcism and healing.

A prime reason for the creation of textiles is clothing. In those regions outside the historical sphere of Indian influence the paramount distinction in the clothing relates to gender: the main female garment is usually a tubular skirt and the basic male form is a flat rectangular textile, either the ancient elongated loincloth or, more commonly in recent centuries, the broader rectangular wrap. This universal differentiation in costume — everyday and ceremonial — reflects the social and cosmological dichotomies and oppositions around which the societies of the Indonesian periphery function. Within these basic forms, certain hierarchies related to clan membership, age, marital status and particularly ritual, maturity and knowledge are often established in colour, motif and intricacy of pattern.

While silk and gold thread textiles intended for ceremonial wear are also woven on a body-tension loom, it features one fundamental variation — the introduction of the reed or comb, a feature that facilitates the separation and control of the finer silk warp threads. Throughout the region the method of inserting the warp threads through the reed during the warping process results in a non-circulating warp, which no longer requires smooth passage around a round warp beam. Instead the unwoven warp threads are rolled out of the way around the broad flat warp beam, often supported by brackets set into solid pedestals, to be released progressively during the weaving process and ultimately to finish as woven fabric rolled tightly onto the breast beam immediately in front of the weaver. The resulting weaving is taken off the loom as a flat length of cloth. This distinction between the circulatory warp of the vegetable fibre textiles and the flat discontinuous silk and gold cloth is both a key to understanding the differences in symbolic significance and conversely the justification for the transformation in meaning. Silk textiles can be exclusive and powerful but they are generally not sacred; the magic of the circular warp found in textiles required for ancestral and animist beliefs is absent.

The essential sacred importance of the ancient vegetable fibre textiles, however, was not necessarily compromised by the development of the new silk complex, even though it exemplified the division of the social structure into ruler and ruled, and between court and village. While the wearing of silk textiles marks crucial status and power distinctions, the continued importance of vegetable fibre textiles with circular warps underlines the essential features of another symbolic system based on more ancient shared understandings about prosperity, a system that was certainly not discarded in the adoption of Indian religions. The ruler and the court still require cotton textiles — textiles with circulating warps woven on back-tension looms without reeds — for ceremonies focusing on ancient beliefs in ancestral intervention, rites in which the essential recognition of gender distinctions for fertility and continuity are universally acknowledged. Thus in Bali the textiles of the aristocracy are dramatic gold and silk brocade or bright weft ikat patterned silks, often displaying overtly Indian images drawn from the great epics or designs from precious imported cloth. However, the *kain wangul* or *bebali*, the soul cloth of any person whether king or commoner, is a simple warp-striped sash, woven from handspun cotton steeped in natural dyes with the uncut continuous circular warp potent with the promise of purifying and exorcising capabilities. The remedy for illness does not lie in the silk and gold *songket*, but in the burning of fragments of the sacred cotton *geringsing*, which, for all the sophistication in technique, is also woven on an ancient form of the continuous warp back-tension loom. The silk textiles are sumptuous but not sacred, fit for a king but not a traditional ritual leader. While the vegetable fibre fabrics disclose precise information about the wearer's origins and status within the microcosm of the village, the gold and silk fabrics distinguish the rulers from the ruled on an international stage.

Throughout the courts of Indonesia the lack of differentiation between male and female textiles is not only striking in the gold and silk woven textiles. The textiles of the Javanese courts are largely created in hand-drawn wax resist batik or by the application of gold leaf or, in the most striking instances, by combining both techniques to create an even more glorious status symbol. Whether the customary rectangular skirtcloths or the huge and voluminous formal court wraps, the form, design and motif are the same for male and female. For aristocratic

women an additional breastcloth was worn in palace ceremonies. (In Bali the breastcloth was also added for temple rites.) This lack of gender differentiation in textile form and ornament is clear on the earliest Hindu and Buddhist sculpture of central Java. It has continued to be displayed on the wooden figures associated with royal marriages. The goddess of fertility, Dewi Sri — the daughter of Batara Guru (Shiva) — and her consort Dewa Sadono (sometimes articulated as the god, Vishnu) are depicted in royal garb with painted patterns articulated in gold leaf; the only differentiating feature is the goddess's breastcloth. In form and design the sculptures mirror the dress of any royal bride and groom.

The most potent of the royal wraps is the *dodot bagun tulak pinarada mas*, a huge dark cotton textile with a brilliant white centre and patterned with gold-leaf glue work, *prada*. The entire indigo-blue section is covered with small gold creatures, some auspicious, some frightening, some real, others imaginary. Elephants, bats, millipedes and scorpions crowd the surface, while the wings of the royal Garuda embellish each corner. As the textile's title suggests, the cloth functions to ward off evil — from the bridal couple, from the monarch and from the realm itself. To this end, the huge royal *dodot bangun tulak* textiles also enshroud the male and female mountain forms (*gunungan*) that are paraded through the central Javanese capital at the Muhaarum celebration of the Prophet Mohammad's birthday. This celebration demonstrates the synthesis that underpins art in Java where images from older cosmological orders — the male–female dualism, the sacred mountain and the protective powers of cloth — are harnessed towards the welfare of the state at an event on the Muslim calendar. The textiles of Java also display this syncretism and ambivalence in numerous ways: a long carrying cloth for a baby, with the royal diagonal 'broken sword' pattern (*parang rusak*) is inscribed with an impassioned prayer to the ancestors, spirits and Allah for a cure of the child's illness. With its inscription written in classical Javanese Sanskrit calligraphy, the textile was clearly created by a desperate family to wrap around and guard a sick child.

While the wearing of gold and silk was widely restricted to members of the nobility across Indonesia, a specific set of sumptuary laws governed the wearing of batik textiles in the courts of Java. Certain patterns were the prerogative of the ruler and his family and these designs were described and illustrated in court inventories. The manner of wearing headcloths and the length of the skirtcloth over breeches was also dictated for court officials. Similar restrictions applied to other textile-related objects including the umbrellas of rank, flags and banners.

Since the wearing of batik in the principalities of Java has been largely restricted to the aristocracy in contrast to the striped homespuns of the peasantry, these regulations govern ceremonial dress within the palace, perceived as it is as a microcosm of the universe. However, the kingdom was also subdivided into regencies, clustered around the royal capital in a mandala pattern, and in each of these centres, away from the omnipotent ruler, similar restrictions and sumptuary laws operated with regards to dress and other regalia. Hence, in the Sultan's palace in Jogjakarta or Surakarta, it was the ruler and his family who wore the largest versions of the restricted patterns; back in his own residence away from the Sultan's palace, however, it would be the regent whose right it was to display the largest motifs in contradistinction to the subordinates of his court.

Many of the restricted batik designs appear to be geometric. Others, such as the *semen* pattern, however, are stylised renditions of the sacred landscape. Although empty of human forms, the designs often feature birds and reptiles animating the layered scenes of mountain ridges and forest foliage, and schematic winged gateways and shrines that are protected by *naga* serpents. On some royal textiles it is the Garuda wings that rise out of the landscape, on others the *naga* are the dominant motif, in confronting pairs or with tails decoratively intertwined. The most symbolic image of royalty is the crowned *naga*, its head ornamented with the classical jewelled headdress of court dancers and noble *wayang* puppet characters. An even more potent version, the winged *naga* simultaneously harnesses the eternal opposition of bird and serpent, and upper and lower layers of the cosmos; the contest of Garuda and *naga* displayed on Balinese court textiles is conflated into one royal motif.

Ancient reptilian motifs associated with the underworld and the female aspects of the cosmos are also manifest in some versions of the *tampan* shipcloths. These may be more than imaginative motifs. Serpent heads have emblazoned the prows of royal ceremonial barges throughout Indonesia; the *naga* ships on the *tampan* may act as a record of this practice among Lampung nobility. Certainly the scenes on the more intricate *tampan* capture the essence of courtly Indonesia: stately ships with royal couples, distinguished not by dress but by differences in size and coiffeur, are placed in pleasure domes, their attendants holding umbrellas and standards on high. They and their aristocratic attendants wear the bulging *dodot* wrap, the hilts of their fine daggers at their waists, their headdress and hairstyles an echo of those worn by royal and supernatural characters in court performances where ancient costume and regalia are also frozen in time. A full gamelan percussion orchestra with gongs and xylophones is laid out on one deck. Other levels of the ships are filled with creatures associated with royalty — elephants, peacocks, horses and griffins. Some riders hold offerings, ceremonial fans and parasols. Even the composite creatures of the sea wear their hair in noble chignon.

The royal journeys — narrative or symbolic — that these scenes depict are now lost. In Java and Bali the *Ramayana* and *Mahabharata* epics are still important sources for models of royal courtly behavior as well as associated imagery. The voyages on the Lampung cloths, however, may be drawn from another set of court literature — the romantic adventures of Prince Panji. An Australian scholar, Adrian Vickers, has drawn parallels between the formal arrangement and content of the square Balinese *malat* painted hangings, which depict Panji scenes, and the pictorial *tampan*. Certainly many of the shipcloths clearly show royal couples at the centre of the shipboard ceremony, and the Panji tales are especially popular throughout the maritime courts of Indonesia.

The scenes on other textiles from Lampung also provide evidence of noble rites, though in a more enigmatic and ambiguous manner. The women's skirts were a feature of transition ceremonies and the imagery embroidered into the bands also encompasses symbols of change. The ship again is the most prevalent, its passengers notable for the radiating headdresses that they appear to wear. While spiky diadems are part of the ceremonial costume of women in some regions of southern and western Sumatra, in Bali they are also a key feature of images of Dewi Sri and her consort, appropriate symbols of fertility and prosperity at many rites of passage, especially marriage and the tooth filings associated with adulthood. Other embroidered images relate to a young man's entry into the adult world: throughout the Malay world bird-shaped palanquins and chariots convey noble boys to their circumcisions and throughout Lampung bridal carriages also display carved bird head 'prows'. These mythical birds appear occasionally on textiles, especially the Lampung *tapis* skirts. Extrapolating to other more obscure motifs in the same bands, it is possible that figures carried on ambiguous square shapes are also being transported in ceremonial procession, possibly on raised platforms or palanquins.

While Javanese and Lampung textiles often contain imagery drawn from ancient court ceremony, Malay textiles, in both gold *songket* and gold leaf, display largely geometric forms, often identified today with local flowers and fruit. So, while the eight-lobed rosette is lotus-like in structure, it is associated with the markings at the base of the mangosteen fruit (*kembang manggis*). However, the continued presence of dragons and other creatures in the ornamental panels across each end of Malay brocades, and the birds and serpents still lurking in the foliated triangular borders are also relics of past figuration. While designs of ships laden with figures of humans and animals flourished for far longer in the south Sumatran hinterland, heavily couched gold-thread embroidered skirts displaying geometric shapes and patterns against dark cotton stripes were often called 'laden junk' (*jung sarat*), indicating that their value and prestige were also tied in the past to nearby trade routes. Textiles from the inland regions of southern Sumatra also share imagery of riders on noble creatures; elephants, buffaloes, horses and other more fanciful animal forms in the borders of certain key textiles from the Lampung region suggest that the role of those textiles in rites of transition continued in colonial times.

Since the Malay cloth-of-gold, the most sumptuous of all silk textiles, was a key symbol of prestige and high social status yet lacked sacred meaning, it could be adapted more readily to changes in fashion and dress. While the upper torsos of Javanese court attendants and performers remained bare, the adoption of Islam in many sultanates and principalities led to the creation of other costume items for ceremonial dress. With no heed to the ancient Southeast Asian strictures — both symbolic and practical — against cutting into cloth, the glamorous jackets and tunics were often embroidered in gold threads on pliable imported silk and velvet, although the stiffer *songket* brocade was also used to create ostentatious upper garments, trousers and headcloths to meet new perceptions of propriety. Moreover, the length of the nobleman's *songket* skirt — another indicator of status — appears to have shortened to expose the rich patterning of the silk and gold trousers beneath.

However, it was the man's headcloth that continued to encapsulate the essence of *songket*. Certain colours and shapes symbolised courtly position, rank and power, and the richness of its gold and ikat dyeing along with the flamboyance, style and originality in the way the headcloth was tied provided members of the elite with the perfect vehicle to shine in the glittering and cosmopolitan company of the Malay court. On the other hand, women rarely wore headcloths on ceremonial occasions in Indonesia. The matrilineal Minangkabau are a notable exception. Only the richly woven wide borders of gold and silver *songket* were exposed in the west Sumatran women's elaborate double-peaked headdresses. The overt references to buffalo horns, also the form of large gold diadems elsewhere on the island, evoke prosperity and fertility. The buffalo is an ancient and widely used symbol of fertility in agricultural communities across the entire Indonesian archipelago. It also appears in gold-couched embroidery and in woven *songket* borders on the textiles of many Lampung cultures.

Embroidery provides a vehicle for non-repetitive fluid and figurative imagery. These attributes are harnessed for the creation of ceremonial hangings, particularly those enclosing seats of honour and bridal thrones. The epic tales of Balinese embroidered hangings have largely been replaced by floral and tree images, although the presence of the Bouraq, the Prophet Mohammad's mount to Heaven, is a graphic reminder of another source of narrative in the Malay courts. The tree image is one of the most pervasive on all forms of Indonesian art, evoking a variety of ancient and fundamental images of an *axis mundi*

between the upper and lower worlds. In courtly regalia it conflates with the sacred mountain into a powerful symbolic form and can be seen in golden offering trees and in *wayang* tree-mountain forms. In the tree branches birds of many types often appear, with jewels, keys, fish and other objects dangling from their beaks.

While the Indian influence in imagery may have diminished, the form has been strengthened: the application of mirror work, the ornamental tongues of cloth, the arrangement of the textiles within the space, even their generic Malay name *tirai*, all suggest cultural influences of the west Indian *toran* hangings.

Many of the early reports of the Indonesian royalty provide the same overwhelming impression: the palaces of Indonesian monarchs were centres of great opulence. The key to this spectacle of wealth and power was in the display of gold regalia, gold furnishings and particularly the gold-embellished garments of the ruler and his courtiers. References to the legacy of the great Hindu-Buddhist empires of Indonesia's golden past were encoded in the parasols of rank, the ceremonies and in styles of dress that vividly distinguished the rulers from the ordinary citizens of their realm.

Further readings

Dumarçay, J, *The Palaces of Southeast Asia: Architecture and Customs*, Oxford University Press, Singapore, 1998.

Gittinger, M, *Splendid Symbols: Textiles and Tradition in Indonesia*, Oxford University Press, Singapore, 1985.

Hall, K, *Maritime Trade and State Development in Early Southeast Asia*, George Allen & Unwin, Sydney, 1985.

Jessup, HI, *Court Arts of Indonesia*, Harry N. Abrams, New York, 1990.

Kartiwa, Suwati et al, *Weaving Dyeing and Embroidery: Diversity in Sumatran Textiles from the Eiko Kusuma Collection*, Fukuoka Art Museum, Fukuoka, 1999.

Leigh, B, *Hands of Time: the Crafts of Aceh*, Djambatan, Jakarta, 1988.

Maxwell, R, *Textiles of Southeast Asia: Tradition, Trade and Transformation*, revised edition, Periplus, Singapore, 2003.

Selvanayagam, G, *Songket: Malaysia's Woven Treasure*, Oxford University Press, Singapore, 1988.

Summerfield, A, Summerfield, J, & Taufik Abdullah (eds), *Walk in Splendor: Ceremonial Dress and the Minangkabau*, Fowler Museum of Cultural History, University of California, Los Angeles, 1999.

Yoshimoto, S, Kain *Perada: The Gold-printed Textiles of Indonesia: Hirayama Collection*, Kodansha, Tokyo, 1988.

(above) Javanese people
Surakarta, Java, Indonesia
Woman's ceremonial breast cloth [*kemben pinarada mas*]   19th century
cotton, gold leaf; stitch-resist dyeing, gold-leaf gluework
51.0 x 232.0 cm
Acquired through gift and purchase from the Collection of
Robert J. Holmgren and Anita Spertus, New York, 2000
2000.984

(below) Javanese people
Surakarta, Java, Indonesia
Royal ceremonial skirt cloth [*dodot bangun tulak alas-alasan pinarada mas*]
late 19th century
cotton, natural dyes, gold leaf; stitch-resist dyeing, gold-leaf gluework
203.0 x 353.0 cm
1984.3167

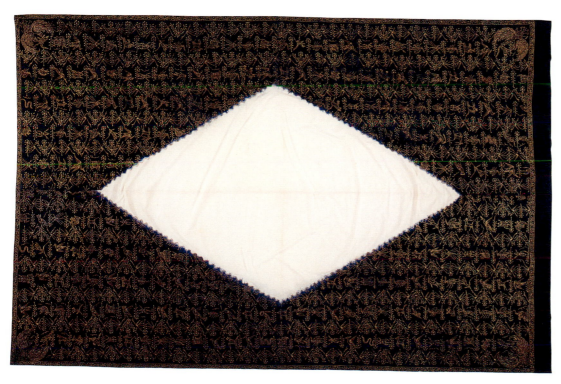

Javanese people
Surakarta, Java, Indonesia
Royal ceremonial skirt cloth [*dodot bangun tuluk alas-alasan pinarada mas*]
19th century
cotton, natural dyes, gold leaf; stitch-resist dyeing, gold-leaf gluework
211.0 x 324.0 cm
Acquired through gift and purchase from the Collection of
Robert J. Holmgren and Anita Spertus, New York, 2000
2000.985

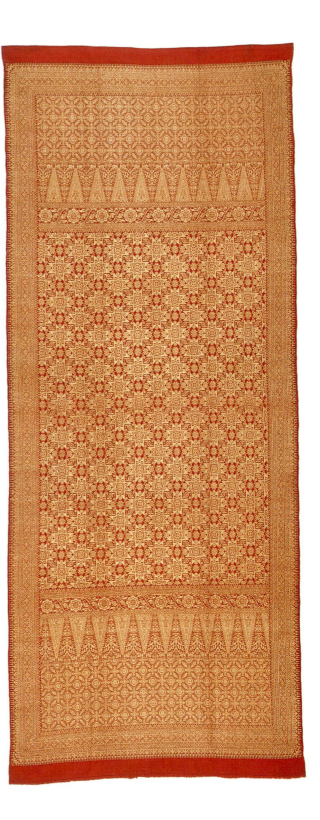

Malay people
Palembang region, south Sumatra, Indonesia
Ceremonial shoulder cloth [*selendang songket lepus rakam*]   19th century
silk, natural dyes, gold thread; supplementary weft weave
260.0 x 84.5 cm
Conserved with the assistance of Di Gregson 1989.497

Malay people
Palembang region, south Sumatra, Indonesia
Ceremonial shoulder cloth [*kain selendang songket*]   19th century
gold thread, silk, natural dyes; supplementary weft weave
222.5 x 89.5 cm
Conserved with the assistance of Pamela Rhemrev 1989.1869

Malay people
Palembang region, south Sumatra, Indonesia
Ceremonial shoulder cloth [*kain selendang songket*]   19th century
gold thread, silk, natural dyes; supplementary weft weave
236.0 x 86.0 cm
1989.1867

Malay people
Palembang region, south Sumatra, Indonesia
Ceremonial shoulder cloth [*kain selendang songket*]   19th century
silk, gold thread, natural dyes; supplementary weft weave
210.0 x 81.0 cm
Conserved with the assistance of Judy Richmond, Canberra, ACT
Gift of Michael and Mary Abbott 1988
1988.1553

Abung people
Lampung, south Sumatra, Indonesia
Ceremonial hanging and heirloom cloth 19th century
silk, cotton, gold thread, natural dyes; supplementary weft weave, embroidery
152.5 x 219.0 cm
1984.1221

(left) Paminggir people
Lampung, south Sumatra, Indonesia
Woman's ceremonial skirt [*tapis*]   19th century
cotton, natural dyes, silk, gold thread, lead-backed mirror pieces;
couching, satin-stitch embroidery, appliqué
106.0 x 67.0 cm
1981.1131

(right) Paminggir people
Lampung, south Sumatra, Indonesia
Woman's ceremonial skirt [*tapis*]   19th century
cotton, natural dyes, silk, gold thread, lead-backed mirror pieces;
couching, satin-stitch embroidery, appliqué
101.0 x 62.0 cm
1981.1132

(opposite above) Malay people
Palembang region, south Sumatra, Indonesia
Ceremonial shoulder cloth [*kain telepok* or *kain prada*]   19th century
silk, natural dyes, gold leaf; stitch-resist dyeing, gold-leaf gluework
210.0 x 85.0 cm
1989.1871

(opposite centre) Malay people
Palembang region, south Sumatra, Indonesia
Ceremonial shoulder cloth [*kain telepok* or *kain prada*]   19th century
silk, natural dyes, gold leaf; gold-leaf gluework, stitch-resist dyeing
83.5 x 213.5 cm
1984.589

(opposite below) Malay people
Palembang, south Sumatra, Indonesia
Ceremonial shoulder cloth [*kain telepok* or *kain prada*]   late 19th – early 20th century
silk, natural dyes, gold leaf; gold-leaf gluework, stitch-resist dyeing
217.0 x 79.0 cm
Gift of Mrs Jeannette Plowright, 2003
2003.224

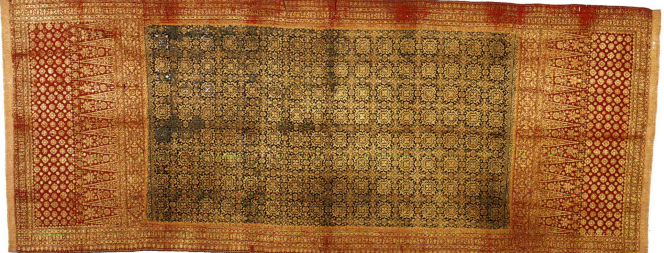

Pasemah region, Sumatra, Indonesia
Ceremonial shoulder or waist cloth early 20th century
cotton, silk, natural dyes, metallic thread; supplementary weft weave
220.0 x 38.0 cm
1981.1133

Pasemah region, Sumatra, Indonesia
Ceremonial shoulder or waist cloth   early 20th century
cotton, metallic thread, natural dyes, silk; supplementary weft weave
230.0 x 34.5 cm
1984.572

Lampung, south Sumatra, Indonesia
Ceremonial textile [*bidak*]   18th century
cotton, silk; embroidery, dip dyeing
278.0 x 74.0 cm
Acquired through gift and purchase from the Collection of
Robert J. Holmgren and Anita Spertus, New York, 2000
2000.902

(above) Pasemah or Bengkulu region, Sumatra, Indonesia
Man's skirt cloth 19th century
cotton, natural dyes, bobbin lace, gold and silver thread;
supplementary weft weave, warp ikat
64.5 x 169.5 cm
1981.1158

(below) Minangkabau people
Solok district, West Sumatra, Indonesia
Shoulder cloth or man's skirt cloth 19th century
silk, gold thread; weft ikat, supplementary weft weave, interlacing
206.0 x 77.0 cm
Acquired through gift and purchase from the Collection of
Robert J. Holmgren and Anita Spertus, New York, 2000
2000.947

(far laft) Minangkabau people
West Sumatra, Indonesia
Woman's head or shoulder cloth [*tengkuluak*
or *kain sandang*]   c. 1880
silk, cotton, gold thread, natural dyes;
supplementary weft weave
141.5 x 78.5 cm
1984.576

(left) Minangkabau people
West Sumatra, Indonesia
Woman's head cloth [*tengkuluak*]   c. 1880
silk, metallic thread; supplementary weft weave
164.0 x 61.0 cm
1984.575

(above) Acehnese people
Aceh, Indonesia
Shoulder or waist cloth [*ija sawa*]   19th century
silk, gold thread; supplementary weft weave
300.0 x 75.0 cm
1987.1060

(right) Minangkabau people
West Sumatra, Indonesia
Ceremonial shoulder cloth [*selendang*]   19th century
silk, gold thread, silver thread, gold gimp; supplementary weft weave
204.0 x 56.0 cm
Acquired through gift and purchase from the Collection of
Robert J. Holmgren and Anita Spertus, New York, 2000
2000.757

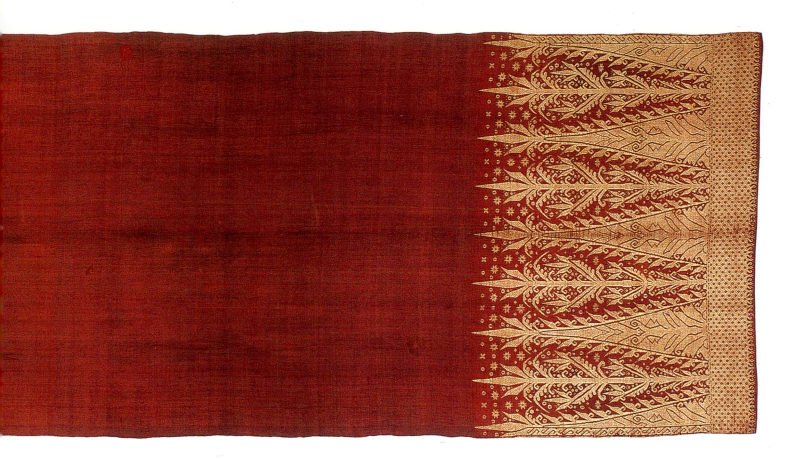

Pasemah region, Sumatra, Indonesia
Shoulder or skirt cloth [*kain bidak*]   19th century
silk, cotton, natural dyes, gold thread; weft ikat, supplementary weft weave
112.0 x 250.0 cm
1980.728

(above) Malay people
Sumatra, Indonesia
Ceremonial hanging [*tirai*] 19th century
cotton, silk, gold thread, lead-backed mirror pieces;
embroidery, appliqué
79.0 x 210 cm
1984.1998

(centre) Acehnese people
Aceh, north Sumatra, Indonesia
Ceremonial hanging [*bi*] early 20th century (detail)
cotton, wool, silk, gold thread, sequins, glass beads, mica;
appliqué, lace, couching, embroidery
64.0 x 208 cm
1984.1986

(below) Malay people
Kalimantan, Indonesia
One of a pair of ceremonial hangings early 20th century
silk, gold metallic thread, sequins; supplementary weft weave, appliq
111.0 x 122.5 cm (brocade only)
1981.1172.a

Malay people
Palembang region, south Sumatra, Indonesia
Man's head cloth [*ikat kepala; tengkuluk*]   19th century
silk, natural dyes, gold thread; weft ikat, supplementary weft weave
86.0 x 84.0 cm
1980.1631

Malay people
Palembang, south Sumatra, Indonesia
Man's head cloth [*ikat kepala; tengkuluk*]   19th century
silk, gold thread; supplementary weft weave, warp and weft ikat
88.0 x 86.5 cm
Conserved with the assistance of Carina Sherlock Enterprises
Acquired through gift and purchase from the Collection of
Robert J. Holmgren and Anita Spertus, New York, 2000
2000.830

Malay people
Palembang, south Sumatra, Indonesia
Ceremonial covering   19th century
silk, gold thread, sequins; embroidery, appliqué
55.0 x 54.0 cm
Acquired through gift and purchase from the Collection of
Robert J. Holmgren and Anita Spertus, New York, 2000
2000.856

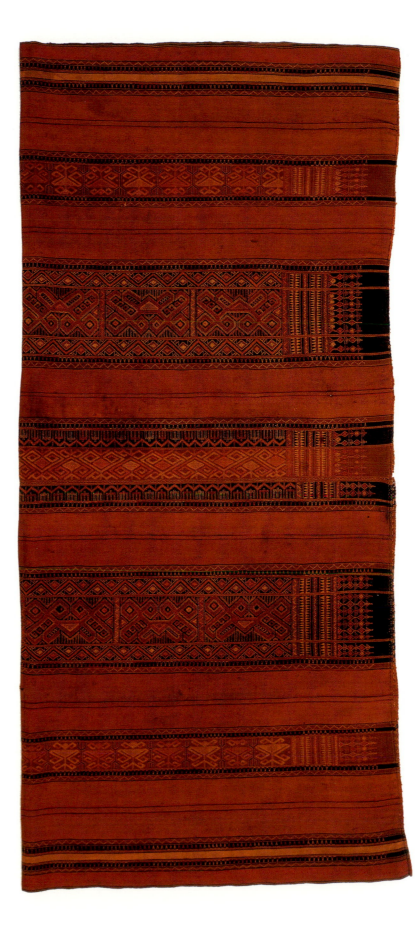

Paminggir or Abung people
Lampung, south Sumatra, Indonesia
Woman's ceremonial skirt [*tapis tusukan ratu*]   19th century
cotton, silk, natural dyes; loom embroidery
107.0 x 122.0 cm
1986.2459

Paminggir or Abung people
Kota Bumi district, Lampung, south Sumatra, Indonesia
Woman's ceremonial skirt [*tapis tusukan ratu*]   19th century
silk, natural dyes; supplementary weft weave, embroidery
134.0 x 110.0 cm
Acquired through gift and purchase from the Collection of
Robert J. Holmgren and Anita Spertus, New York, 2000
2000.803

Abung or Paminggir people
Lampung, south Sumatra, Indonesia
Woman's ceremonial skirt [*tapis*]   19th century
silk, cotton, mica; supplementary weft weave, embroidery, couching
141.0 x 123.0 cm
Acquired through gift and purchase from the Collection of
Robert J. Holmgren and Anita Spertus, New York, 2000
2000.774

Paminggir people
Lampung, south Sumatra, Indonesia
Woman's ceremonial skirt [*tapis*]   19th century
cotton, silk, natural dyes, mirror pieces;
warp ikat, embroidery
128.0 x 118.7 cm
1981.1125

(above) Semawa or Bimanese people
Sumbawa, Indonesia
Shoulder cloth or man's hip cloth [*salampe* or *pabasa*] 1900–1925 (detail)
silk, dyes; tapestry weave, supplementary weft weave
339.0 x 69.0 cm
1984.1253

(below) Malay people
Palembang, south Sumatra, Indonesia
Shoulder cloth [*selendang*] 19th century (detail)
silk, sequins, gold thread, dyes; weft ikat, stitch-resist dyeing, embroidery, appliqué
193.5 x 81.0 cm
Acquired through gift and purchase from the Collection of
Robert J. Holmgren and Anita Spertus, New York, 2000
2000.782

(left above) Malay people
Palembang, south Sumatra, Indonesia
Ceremonial vest mid 19th century
silk, gold thread, sequins, cotton; couching, appliqué, button-hole stitch
51.0 x 51.0 cm
Conserved with the assistance of Canberra Region Feltmakers
Acquired through gift and purchase from the Collection of
Robert J. Holmgren and Anita Spertus, New York, 2000
2000.866

(left below) Malay people
Palembang, south Sumatra, Indonesia
Nobleman's ceremonial trousers 19th century
silk, gold thread, sequins; supplementary weft weave, embroidery
96.0 x 58.0 cm
Acquired through gift and purchase from the Collection of
Robert J. Holmgren and Anita Spertus, New York, 2000
2000.935

(opposite from top to bottom)
Javanese people
Central Java, Indonesia
Man's ceremonial jacket [*baju prada*] 19th century
cotton, gold leaf; gold-leaf gluework
58.4 x 179.6 cm
1988.1547

Bengkulu or Komering region
Sumatra, Indonesia
Jacket 19th century
cotton, gold thread; supplementary warp weave, supplementary
weft weave, embroidery
39.0 x 140.0 cm
Acquired through gift and purchase from the Collection of
Robert J. Holmgren and Anita Spertus, New York, 2000
2000.891

Kauer people
South Sumatra, Indonesia
Unmarried woman's ceremonial jacket c. 1900–1930
cotton, silk, natural dyes, cowrie shell, gold thread, mirror pieces;
supplementary weft weave, embroidery, appliqué
23.5 x 152.0 cm
1981.1170

Kauer people
South Sumatra, Indonesia
Unmarried woman's ceremonial jacket c. 1900–1930
cotton, natural dyes, cowrie shells, gold thread, mirror pieces, silk;
embroidery, appliqué, supplementary weft weave,
32.0 x 150.0 cm
1980.1652

(left) Abung people
Lampung, south Sumatra, Indonesia
Woman's ceremonial skirt [*tapis tua*] 1900–1940
cotton, natural dyes, gold thread, metallic tinsel, sequins;
couching, embroidery, appliqué
103.0 x 59.0 cm
1980.729

(opposite above) Kulawi district, Sulawesi, Indonesia
Woman's ceremonial tunic [*halili petondo*] c. 1910
cotton, mica, sequins; embroidery, appliqué
57.0 x 92.0 cm
Acquired through gift and purchase from the Collection of
Robert J. Holmgren and Anita Spertus, New York, 2000
2000.716

(opposite below) Kulawi district, Sulawesi, Indonesia
Woman's ceremonial tunic [*halili petondo*] c. 1920
cotton, gold ribbon, mica, paint; embroidery, appliqué
59.0 x 91.0 cm
Acquired through gift and purchase from the Collection of
Robert J. Holmgren and Anita Spertus, New York, 2000
2000.697

(below left) Malay people
Palembang, south Sumatra, Indonesia
Ceremonial pillow end [*muka bantal*]   19th century
satin, gold thread, mirror; embroidery, couching, appliqué
9.0 x 17.0 cm
Acquired through gift and purchase from the Collection of
Robert J. Holmgren and Anita Spertus, New York, 2000
2000.918

(below right) Malay people
Palembang, south Sumatra, Indonesia
Ceremonial pillow end [*muka bantal*]   19th century
satin, gold thread, mirror; embroidery, couching, appliqué
12.0 x 20.0 cm
Acquired through gift and purchase from the Collection of
Robert J. Holmgren and Anita Spertus, New York, 2000
2000.894

(above) Malay people
Palembang, south Sumatra, Indonesia
Ceremonial cushion [*bantal*]   19th century
kapok, cotton, velvet, silk, gold thread, sequins; embroidery, couching
56.0 x 35.0 x 7.0 cm
1986.2455

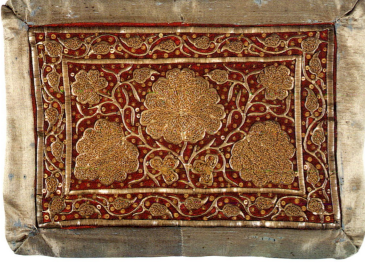

Balinese people
Bali, Indonesia
Ceremonial breast cloth [*kain perada*]   late 19th – early 20th century
cotton, natural dyes, gold leaf; batik, gold-leaf gluework
53.5 x 272.0 cm
Gift of Michael and Mary Abbott 1987
1987.1081

(below) Malay people
Palembang region, south Sumatra, Indonesia
One of a pair of ceremonial pillow ends [*muka bantal*]   20th century
gold tinsel, sequins, cotton, velvet; appliqué, couching, embroidery
15.5 x 25.0 cm
Gift of Michael and Mary Abbott 1991
1991.587

4 THE FABRIC OF TRADE
Indian textiles

Despite the significant impact of Indian symbols of religion and statecraft, an ancient and far more pervasive interchange in textile designs can be directly attributed to commerce, for the long saga of Indian and Indonesian textile exchanges is inseparable from the history of the international spice trade. Imperial embassies, petty traders, adventurers and company bureaucrats were drawn to the ports of India and the islands of Indonesia by the lure of cloves, nutmeg and mace and the desire for profit. Christopher Columbus's famous discovery of the Americas in 1492 was financed by the monarchs of Spain, eager to become the European leaders in the quest for the riches of the East.

Had Columbus secured his aim of reaching the Asian spice islands by sailing west, as compatriot Ferdinand Magellan successfully achieved some 30 years later, he would have been much disappointed by his lack of the key commodity in that trade, Indian textiles. A primary element in the elaborate centuries-old barter system that had developed around the produce of the East Indies was cloth acquired at various Indian centres in Gujarat, Bengal and along the Coromandel coast, and also in the busy Southeast Asian entrepots of Aceh, Malacca, Banten and Makassar. Even when the Europeans did succeed in entering the spice trade they continued to be surprised at the strength of the demand for Indian cloth, and the specificity of the tastes of regional markets for certain types, colours and designs of textiles.

There are many reasons for the enormous appeal of the Indian textiles. It lay in large part in the very nature of the textiles themselves. Across

(opposite) Coromandel coast, India
Traded to Bali, Indonesia
Heirloom hanging [*palampore*] late 17th century (detail)
cotton, natural dyes, mordants; mordant painting
164.0 x 106.0 cm
Gift of Cecilia Ng in memory of Anthony Forge
2002.152

the archipelago women were undoubtedly already skilled weavers of vegetable fibre textiles and makers of beaten bark-cloth. However, the materials and techniques from which the Indian cloths were made were clearly sensational. So too was the size of the fabrics: many of the complete textiles traded to the Indonesian region were 5 to 6 metres in length and nearly a metre wide (similar dimensions to the modern Indian *sari*). Indian weavers were also producing full bolts of cotton cloth, in sheer muslins and rugged calico. In contrast, even when cotton was widely cultivated locally, especially in the drier parts of the archipelago, Indonesian weavers continued to use the ancient back-tension loom. And although in parts of central and western Indonesia the hand-operated spinning wheel sometimes replaced the drop-spindle, the needs of sacred cloth for ancestral rituals appear to have enshrined long-standing and culturally conservative textile techniques. The introduction of Sanskrit-based terminology for both 'cotton' (*kapas*, from the Sanskrit *karpasa*) and 'spinning wheel' (*jantra*, from the Indian *cakra*, wheel) indicates early Indian origins for technologies and materials rather than literary origins probably unconnected to the burgeoning trade in textiles.

A range of Indian textile types, including tie-dyes, embroideries and brocade weaves, appears to have been popular in the East. The trade records also tell us that plain dyed, striped and checked cottons were in large demand; evidence of these textiles sometimes survives as the foundation fabric of beaded and embroidered garments, hangings and other objects. However, most of those textiles that do survive to tell the tale of extraordinarily long and varied journeys fall into two categories: mordant-painted or block-printed cottons, and double ikat silks.

The most highly prized textiles across the entire Indonesian archipelago were the double ikat *patola* (singular *patolu*, but since the plural term is widely used throughout Indonesia to mean both singular and plural it will be used here in the same manner). The amazing silk textiles – usually 5-metre *sari*-size lengths of luminous colour – were then only produced in Gujarat in west India, and now only in one town, Patan. Patterned by separately tying and dyeing the weft and the warp threads into intricate designs before weaving, the textiles are among the most admired, most prestigious and most expensive both within India and in Indonesia. A luxury textile in India, they are closely associated with religious and communal celebrations. In Gujarat, where *patola* are still woven, it is notably associated with fertility: sheltering shrines for the Mother Goddess, covering a bridegroom's horse and, most spectacularly, worn as wedding *sari* by brides and their mothers. The characteristic patterning of the *patola*, however, also survives on the painted walls of temple niches and the clothing of Hindu deities in regions of southern India. In Indonesia, their brilliant colours, luminosity and sheen, along with the intricacy of the resist dyeing of both the warp and weft threads into complex designs (which spring to life only during the weaving process) meant that the silk textiles were the favourite of rulers and shamans alike. The limited range of motifs and the standard design format did nothing to detract from the enduring appeal of the double ikat *patola*.

Occasionally found with striking plain centres, especially when for domestic Indian patrons, but more usually covered with gem-like patterns, the *patola* are framed along both sides with distinctive combinations of plain and narrow ikat stripes. The end panels vary, with those made especially for export to Indonesia often displaying the distinctive rows of triangles. Bands of triangles are found in all Indonesian art forms – stone, wood, metal, pigments and textiles – from the earliest remnants of ancestral cultures through the Hindu-Buddhist period to objects from Islamic communities. Their presence on *patola* that have survived across the entire arc of islands suggests that this was a feature much admired by all Indonesian clients. Few of the *patola* that reached Indonesia have the bands of interwoven gold metallic thread in the *pallav*, the end of the textile exposed when the cloth is draped as a *sari*.

Indian artisans, particularly it seems those of west India, had long been producing for international markets. From the time of the Indus valley civilisation in the third millennium BC, indigo and madder-red dyed cottons had been created on the Indian sub-continent for foreign customers. Fragments of Indian indigo cotton batik dating from as early as the 6th century AD have been discovered in China at sites along the ancient Silk Road. Large numbers of Indian cotton fragments – decorated with mordanted dyes and batik stamp resist – have been found at the old Islamic port of Fustat on the Nile delta in Egypt and in coastal sites along the Red Sea, evidence of a vigorous trade to the Middle East spanning at least 500 years from the beginning of the second millennium of the present era.

Cotton textiles decorated by the same techniques, sometimes with identical designs, have been found in many locations across the Indonesian archipelago in recent decades. Unlike the small fragments recovered from the Egyptian excavation, these have not been buried but have survived, often in excellent condition, in safe storage in some of the more inaccessible parts of modern Indonesia. Since the dominant dye used, whether with block-printed or hand-drawn mordants, was the colour-fast 'Turkey red' chay or madder, the designs still appear with surprising boldness despite their considerable age. In this decorative process, the application of chemically different liquid mordants to the surface of the cotton cloths – either with a series of carved wooden blocks or a slim pen-like instrument – resulted in design elements of different colours when combined with the same dye substance. In particular, iron oxide mordants created black dyes and potassium oxide led to bright red colour. Other substances and combinations resulted in browns and purples. Many of the same textiles were also coloured blue in indigo vats, the undyed sections protected from the blue dyes by the application of batik resists.

During the colonial period, the Indian luxury silks were much noted. Local rulers sympathetic to the Dutch plans for the region were provided with visual symbols of their loyalty – Indian trade textiles and silver and gold staffs and medallions. This bestowal of significant and valuable textiles and other precious objects was also made in other districts to the chiefs of dominant clans who, by acknowledging Dutch suzerainty, were invested as *raja*, establishing a hereditary nobility where once the balance of power had been shared between the largest and most powerful clans. In these instances, Indian trade cloths, particularly the beautiful silk *patola*, were the prerogative of the rulers and a symbol of their power and prestige. This was the case, for example, on the island of Roti, where each year the Governor-General of the Netherlands East Indies conveyed his continuing support for the local princes through gifts that included trade cloths. These presentations were in fact prompted by the Rotinese rulers themselves, who sent formal requests for the *patola* (along with silver staffs and gin!) annually to the colonial capital, Batavia.

The brilliant *patola* also continued to be ostentatiously displayed in the principalities of Java, whose rulers acted as regents for the Dutch colonial government. In palace pageant the double ikat silks were very much in evidence: as skirtcloths and long trousers, waist sashes and shoulder pieces, cushion covers and curtains; on members of the royal family, their courtiers and attendants, and bridal effigies of princes and princesses; and in *wayang* theatre on all manner of puppets and performers. It is thus not surprising that the Indian cotton cloths most often recorded displayed designs that replicated the double ikat silks. Ironically, in quite a number of instances these cotton counterparts have remained the only signal to popular *patola* designs of the past that have now been lost.

The lack of memory of the many other types of Indian cotton imports mentioned in the extensive records of the European trading companies was very strange and, because those textiles had not survived in museum and ethnological records, their importance to Indonesian textile history was largely overlooked. During the intervening centuries, however, many highly prized Indian cotton and silk textiles have been safely preserved, secreted in village treasuries across Indonesia. The small-scale nature of the societies that had valued and cared for the textiles, often key objects in ceremony, ensured that they had seldom if ever been observed by outsiders. Moreover, in the 20th century many of the ancestral practices associated with these clan heirlooms were the target of missionary zeal (both Muslim and Christian) and sacred objects from the older belief systems were systematically destroyed, as were the clan temples and shrines in which they were housed.

In the last two decades of the 20th century, however, the amazing variety of Indian imported cottons has gradually become evident, encompassing designs inspired by domestic Indian models, as well as motifs and styles specifically created for international markets including Indonesia. The study of these imported textiles not only throws new light on the history of Indonesian design but also provides a crucial resource for re-evaluating Indian textile history.

From their entrance into the Indian Ocean trade arena, the Western traders sought ways to dominate the Eastern spice trade. To ensure the regular, reliable flow of the Indian textile currency, and to inhibit competition, the European trading companies established strategic textile producing and shipping centres throughout the Indian subcontinent to order, supervise, store and export the huge quantities of Indian fabric needed in their commercial ventures. As part of the bureaucratisation and control of cloth and production, company identification was stamped on many textiles. The presence of the black VOC initials of the United Dutch East India Company (*Veerenigde Oost-Indische Compagnie*) on the ends of many textiles found in Indonesia confirmed a 17th- or 18th-century dating. As a result art historians tended to extrapolate 17th- to 18th-century dates for all Indian trade textiles found across the archipelago, assuming that they too were traded at the height of the European mercantile period.

In this same era European enthusiasm for the fine muslins and colourfast chintzes of India was gaining momentum: designs of flowering trees, floral bouquets and leafy tendrils dominated the trade in cotton cloth to the West. These floral patterns also found their way east where again they were much admired. A considerable number of large *palampore* chintz textiles, with striking hand-drawn asymmetric arboreal motifs in vivid colours, have survived, especially in Lampung, central Sulawesi, Bali and Lombok. As in the stately homes of England, some have been used as hangings. Other lengths of chintz were stitched into regional clothing, as also occurred in the Netherlands. Throughout Indonesia, however, they were particularly popular as canopies for ceremonies, protecting the events taking place beneath in supernatural and practical ways; as such they were often known as *lelangit* or *lelehur*, ambiguous references to their physical, symbolic and spiritual connections with the heavens and the ancestors.

European fashions demanded changes in patterns, colours and arrangements on almost an annual basis during the craze for Indian chintz. The parallels between dated examples in Western collections and ones located in Indonesia resulted in some quite precise attributions: one flowering tree cloth stored in the Sulawesi hinterland can be dated stylistically to the Dutch enterprises at Petaboli on the Coromandel coast circa 1725. Yet while the shifts in border swags and floral bouquets can be recognised on many Indonesian heirlooms, in other cases the tree design on textiles destined for the East became rather rigid and generic, striking when floating above the glow of evening lamps at sacred rites but without the delicate pen-work that distinguished the greatest Indian *kalamkari* textiles. (The generic Indian term for pen (*qalam* or *kalam*) and work (*kari*) was rarely adopted in Indonesia, although in Lombok, for example, a local term for the flowering tree heirlooms is *kalangkali*.) This in no way appears to have diminished the attraction of this genre of designs.

Other textiles were very Hindu Indian in form and features, the most notable being the large scenes of the *Ramayana* battle. Against a plain white background the large figures of the main protagonists — Rama and Ravana — confront each other while their embattled supporters leap and grapple each other amid flying arrows and severed limbs in a rather chaotic arrangement. The style of costume and depiction of the characters, the freehand though often crude drawing, and the epic subject matter all point to origins in south Indian temple hangings. The *Ramayana* cloths were certainly popular in Hindu Bali, but surprisingly more survive among the sacred ancestral heirlooms of the animist Toraja. Similarly another unusual textile in south Indian temple style, displaying a ferocious double-headed bird devouring elephants, has been stored for centuries in a village treasury on the island of Timor where its protective appeal differs greatly from the Indian designer's intent.

The very long horizontal Indian hangings depicting the Hindu goddess Durga and the elephant-headed deity Ganesha were most admired in the southeast Moluccas in far eastern Indonesia, where they form a special and ambiguous category of the sacred valuables; although not far from the original source of the famed spices, these islands today are very far from the main conduits of communication. Large numbers of Indian cotton textiles survive in the remote islands as items of great value in a traditional hierarchy of objects, occasionally worn draped around a performer in a ceremony, but playing a key role in bride wealth exchanges at marriage, as well as for paying ritual debts. In contrast to the universal association of textiles with femaleness, however, recognition of their exotic foreign origins sometimes places them in the male category of valuables, to be balanced by locally made textiles in any important ceremonial display or exchange.

Known generically as *basta*, from the west Indian term *bafta* (meaning 'woven' in Persian), which was adopted internationally as the trade term for plain calico from Gujarat, in the south Moluccas the local term covers all types of Indian imported cloth — figurative, geometric-patterned and plain red or blue. Such shifts in terminology across cultures and time are widely found. Perhaps the most confusing is the application of the term *cindé*. Like its English counterpart *chintz* and its Dutch parallel *sits*, *cindé* is usually applied to various mordant-painted (and block-printed) Indian cotton textiles, especially those originating on the Coromandel coast. In Java, however, *cindé* is the word for double ikat silks, known elsewhere in the archipelago by various *patola*-related terms including *katipa*.

Some of the designs displayed on the Indian cottons created some unease among art historians. Patterns identical or very similar to those on the fragments found at Fustat have been noted. Most famous was the design of geese encircling a central roundel: it had become a signature of the Fustat discoveries in the 1930s and the appearance of the sacred goose (*hamsa*) patterns on a number of very large textiles, some complete 5-metre lengths, in the Toraja region of Sulawesi caused great excitement. So too did a number of other *ma'a* (*mawa*) or *mbesa* as these Indian imported treasures are known to the various peoples of the mountainous hinterland of Sulawesi. Rare treasures displayed large female figures arranged across cloths of 5 to 6 metres in size. Even more rare were the hunting or court narratives in a double frieze arrangement stretching the length of each cloth. The style and the content of each scene with noblemen on elephants, the hunters on horseback, noblewomen with attendants, the accoutrements of the courts including ornamental canopies, and the patterning on the costume (like the parrots and crested *hamsa* goose design) resonate with the paintings of late 14th- and 15th-century west India. In particular the device for depicting the faces of human figures with the

second eye protruding from behind an otherwise flat two-dimensional profile was a characteristic feature of the illuminated manuscripts of the Jain artists of Gujarat from that period.

These apparent anomalies between style and the accepted 17th- to 18th-century dating were explained by the conservatism of textiles where patterns might remain popular although a style might no longer be in vogue. Moreover, where production was for export, the tastes of distant markets might reflect little of the intervening changes in style in domestic Indian art. Recent developments in radiocarbon-14 dating, however, have partly solved the mystery. The quantity of carbon required in Accelerated Mass Spectroscopy (AMS) dating is now very small, which means that the amount of the organic object required for accurate testing is greatly reduced: museums that were once understandably reluctant to destroy a considerable part of an artefact can now use this exciting technique on suitable targets with minimal damage. A number of those textiles in the mediaeval west-Indian painting style have been found to have been produced contemporaneously with the manuscripts, with dates spanning from the early 14th to early 15th century, for example, for one extremely rare hunting scene.

Another textile in west-Indian painting style has been very convincingly dated by John Guy in his 1998 book *Woven Cargoes: Indian Textiles in the East*. His argument is based on large maker's seals on one end of the 5.34-metre-long textile, which features a series of 12 female court attendants, each with a different costume and accoutrements. The seals indicate that the cloth was made in AD 1500 during the rule of Muhamad Shah (r. 1459–1511), making it, as Guy points out, the earliest inscribed, dated Indian textile recorded in Indonesia and a critical document in the dating of textiles of this type.

The designs on the vast majority of decorative Indian textiles — whether *patola* or chintz — were continuous patterns of stars and rosettes, of grids and trellises, of flowers and tendrils and of abstract and geometric forms. The popularity in Indonesia of this genre of patterning owed much to an admiration of the great and powerful Islamic courts of India, Persia and Turkey: their rich vocabulary of ornament and the focus on exquisite decorative arts resonated with the desire of the Indonesian kingdoms to embrace a more Islamic and international style. The Indian makers responded to international and local trends incorporating popular European floral and fruit designs, and Islamic arabesques and lamps, as well as patterns that imitated other textile techniques — woven motifs were represented by small blocks of colour and spots were used to represent tie-dyeing. Some patterns can be identified in domestic Indian art, others also proved popular with Western or Japanese markets. While the *patola* were always carefully framed with elaborate end borders, many of the cotton lengths were covered in overall patterning, possibly intended in other markets to be tailored into garments. Many survive intact in Indonesia.

The structure of many textile designs, however, appears to have been created specifically for an Indonesian clientele. The popular design structure of the *patola* was also applied to cotton cloths, although invariably the market taste for shorter *kain panjang* or *sarong* lengths predominated. The most common format of Indian textiles, in cotton or silk, in *sari-* or *sarong-*size lengths, comprises a patterned field, often arranged in a square grid, with narrow decorative borders along each side of the cloth merging into wide elaborate end panels dominated by rows of triangles. These distinctive end designs and the delicate border ribbons are usually filled with tendrils and arabesques, although rabbits, lace filigree and even double-headed Hapsburg eagles have been borrowed from repertoires of other international markets. Occasionally local rulers added status to treasured objects by embellishing them with gold, isolating and highlighting the brilliant hues of the underlying patterned chintz.

In trade the term *sarasa* was widely applied to these textiles, including the more specific *sarasa patola*. Throughout western and central Indonesia *sembagi* was also applied to the cotton textiles of this characteristic format. Both terms remain part of Indonesian vocabulary although they retain specific regional meanings. A large cloth type was also created specifically for Sumatra and Java: it comprises two mirror designs stitched together to form a huge rectangle. This follows the form of the royal Javanese *dodot* wrap, and its appearance in the Lampung treasuries may well reflect the centuries-old Javanese suzerainty over that region. However, the damage caused by tabs and ties in each corner of these textiles indicates that these may also have functioned as canopies or hangings in other ceremonial contexts.

The remarkable endurance of these early Indian textiles in remote rural Indonesia can only be explained by the admiration for and, in many cases, the veneration of fine textiles in most Indonesian cultures. Whether local and imported, whether made by highly esteemed local experts or created by deified ancestors, the ownership and control of fine textiles adds to the prestige and power of clan leaders, aristocratic families and royal households. Conversely their loss or deterioration is an omen of impending disaster. In particular it is only through the crucial role the exotic Indian objects play in the many ceremonies of religion and state throughout the entire Indonesian archipelago that the survival of so many fine examples can be understood. From one tip of the archipelago to the other — from Aceh to Papua — Indian textiles can be found in ceremonies of state, in exchanges of valuables, in the sacred heirlooms of clan temples and palace strongholds. They were often ranked at the peak of the totality of a culture's textiles,

above the most exquisite local creations. In east Flores and the Solor archipelago, further hierarchies were established within categories of cloth — local and Indian. Thus it was often the Indian textiles that were the symbols of the most prestigious union of clans in marriage and conspicuous at the funerals of great leaders. In marriage arrangements the gift of buffalo and other cattle, and of valuable goods such as gold jewellery and ivory tusk from the extended family of the groom were counterbalanced by the finest female objects from the bride's relatives — superb textiles. While there had long been a graduated system of gifts of locally woven textiles, the Indian cloths appear to have displaced the finest and most intricate warp ikat fabrics at the top of the scale. The superior rank of the *patola* over the finest locally woven *hinggi* is demonstrated at important funerals, where the body of a prominent Sumba leader is shrouded in the Indian silk ikat.

Since the wellbeing of Indonesian societies hung on the quality and quantity of textiles — local and exotic — local skills for their preservation were well developed. Textiles were interlaced with powerful herbs and fragrant leaves, hung from rafters by a fine cord, placed in chests lined with aromatic woods, and stored in the lofts of clan houses where they were protected by ancestors and rat-deterring disks; these methods were combined to amazing success. Annual ceremonies in which heirlooms and regalia were paraded, aired, cleansed and blessed ensured that any deterioration would be caught in time. Their regular appearance in the cycle of rites, and their careful seclusion between those ceremonies, appears to have safely balanced their exhibition and conservation.

The trade in Indian fabrics to Southeast Asia reached its peak in the 17th and 18th centuries, before the late 18th-century decline of the trading companies in the face of industrialisation in Europe, and the lack of interest in the traditional commodities of trade. Refrigeration replaced spices for preserving foodstuff, aniline dyes replaced natural barks and leaves, and gold was discovered far from the East Indies. While European interest in India and Indonesia remained, the colonies were to become fertile fields for plantation production and markets for industrial Europe. The ancient connections between India and Indonesia were effectively severed.

Yet the importance of Indian textiles in Indonesian ceremony continued unabated. The wellbeing of Indian heirloom treasures became a thermometer for the wellbeing of the whole community. In many parts of Flores, for example, the state of the village or clan *patola* was assessed before certain activities were undertaken; if, when unwrapped, it was discovered to be in torn and fragile condition, then it forebode ill for the approaching agricultural season, or the coming of the rains, and human and natural tragedies threatened village and family. On the other hand if the *patola* emerged from its storage place in fine condition, the immediate future would be prosperous. The capacity of these magical objects to heal themselves was matched by their powers to heal individual illness or communal epidemics, and to ward off evil when wrapped around a sick child or clan regalia. Where not all families owned such treasures, they were sometimes loaned out when occasions required it — an illness among the extended kin, or a wedding at a distant hamlet.

In the case of the Toraja peoples of Sulawesi in whose care many of the most spectacular Indian cotton cloths have rested over the centuries, the imported *mawa*, along with local counterparts made in emulation of the highly regarded imports, constitute sacred heirlooms, believed to have been created in a distant past by important, sometimes mythological ancestors who possessed skills now lost to even the most experienced makers of textiles in living memory. (This is perhaps not surprising since mordant painting and printing has never been practised in Indonesia, where other techniques produce the finest local cloth. Toraja weavers, for example, are best known for their huge warp ikat cottons in bold geometric patterns.)

Textiles are essential for the successful playing out of Toraja ritual and, like the rites themselves, the cloths are divided into two types: those associated with the activities of life and those required for the ceremonies of death. In such a fundamental division, it is local textiles, especially the great warp ikats, that serve as shrouds for the deceased and enclose and protect the thousands of guests who pour into villages to participate in the elaborate funeral ceremonies for which the Toraja are widely famous. Scores (sometimes even hundreds) of buffalo are slaughtered in celebration of the passage of a local leader from this world to the next where he or she will join the formidable array of ancestors who can still manipulate the world of the living. In parts of the Toraja region where graves, not cliff-face tombs, are the place where bodies are interred, local warp ikat textiles enwrap the grave architecture, warding off evil.

In contrast, the rites of life — associated with agriculture and prosperity, planting and harvest festivals, and marriage and fertility — are quarantined from the ceremonies of death. The expensive funerals are planned for months, sometimes years in advance, and are never scheduled at times devoted to crucial agricultural activities. The textiles associated with these rites of life are the sacred *mawa* (or *ma'a*), the heirloom treasures stored in the roofs of the great clan houses, the most holy section of the construction. Most of the *mawa* are centuries-old imported Indian cloth. In one of the most spectacular displays of the role of these textiles and their male counterparts, swords and knives, the Toraja build a huge stairway, the *bate* — a bamboo ladder to which hundreds of rolls of Indian textiles are attached, interspersed with ancient swords and machetes. This structure towers above the proceedings, a symbolic invitation to the ancestors to descend and join the participants in celebrations of the rites of life.

Despite the enormous care taken to preserve and guard these heirlooms, the life span of such fragile objects is limited. Subtle shifts in their use have extended that life span: the dead may be draped in a *patola* but not buried with it; the elaborate negotiations of bride wealth may be illusionary rather than physical as no objects actually change hands in the carefully balanced circulation of brides, gifts and counter-gifts. The power of small fragments of trade cloth is harnessed — the fragments burnt to produce healing balms where conventional medical practice fails to cure in Hindu Bali, stitched as ornamental panels into ceremonial garments in Christian Sulawesi, and tied into the fringes of *tumbal* banners as a spiritual tool to achieve a desired end in Islamic Lombok.

The most reliable way to secure the power and majesty of trade cloth imagery was to transfer symbols and motifs onto local textiles. This transposition of what were perceived to be key elements of the many and varied Indian designs would prove to be strangely eclectic and enormously creative as Indonesian textile artists attempted to conserve the vital essence of their sacred treasures. So successful were some of these local transformations that they ultimately superseded the Indian textiles in the theatre of local and even international trade.

Further readings

Barnes, R, *Indian Block-printed Textiles in Egypt: The Newberry Collection in the Ashmolean*, Oxford, 2 vols, Clarendon Press, Oxford, 1997.
Bühler, A, & E Fischer, *The Patola of Gujarat*, 2 vols, Krebs AG, Basel, 1979.
Bühler, A, & E Fischer, *The Chintz Collection: The Calico Museum of Textiles, India*, 2 vols, Calico Museum, Ahmedabad, 1983.
Crill, R, *Indian Ikat Textiles*, V & A Publications, London, 1998.
de Jonge, N, *The Forgotten Islands of Indonesia*, Periplus, Singapore, 1995.
Gittinger, M, *Master Dyers to the World: Technique and Trade in Early Indian Dyed Cotton Textiles*, The Textile Museum, Washington, D.C., 1982.
Guy, J, 'Sarasa and Patola: Indian Textiles in Indonesia', *Orientations*, vol. 20, no. 1, 1989.
Guy, J, *Woven Cargoes: Indian Textiles in the East*, Thames and Hudson, London, 1998.
Holmgren, RJ, & AE Spertus, 'Newly Discovered Patolu Motif Types — Extensions to Alfred Bühler and Eberhard Fischer (1979), The Patola of Gujarat', in Völger, G, & K von Welck (eds), *Indonesian Textiles*, Ethnologica, Cologne, 1991.
Yoshioka, T, & S Yoshimoto, *Sarasa of the World*, Kyoto Shoin, Kyoto, 1980.

Coromandel coast, India
Traded to Palembang region, Sumatra, Indonesia
Ceremonial cloth and sacred heirloom [*kain sembagi*]   17th–18th century
cotton, natural dyes, mordants, gold leaf;
mordant block printing, gold-leaf gluework, painting, batik
115.0 x 263.5 cm
1981.1165

Rajasthan, India
Traded to Java, Indonesia
Ceremonial umbrella for royalty [*payung*]   20th century
silk, sequins, gold thread, cotton, chrome-plated steel; embroidery, couching, appliqué
122.0 x 170.0 cm
1987.1545

Gujarat, India
Traded to Sulawesi, Indonesia
Ceremonial cloth and sacred heirloom [*ma'a*]   18th century
cotton, natural dyes, mordants; mordant painting, batik, supplementary weft weave,
stitching
190.0 x 700.0 cm
1984.3176

Coromandel coast, India
Traded to Sulawesi, Indonesia
Ceremonial cloth and sacred heirloom [*ma'a*]   18th century (detail)
handspun cotton, natural dyes, mordants; mordant painting, batik
106.0 x 487.0 cm
1991.630

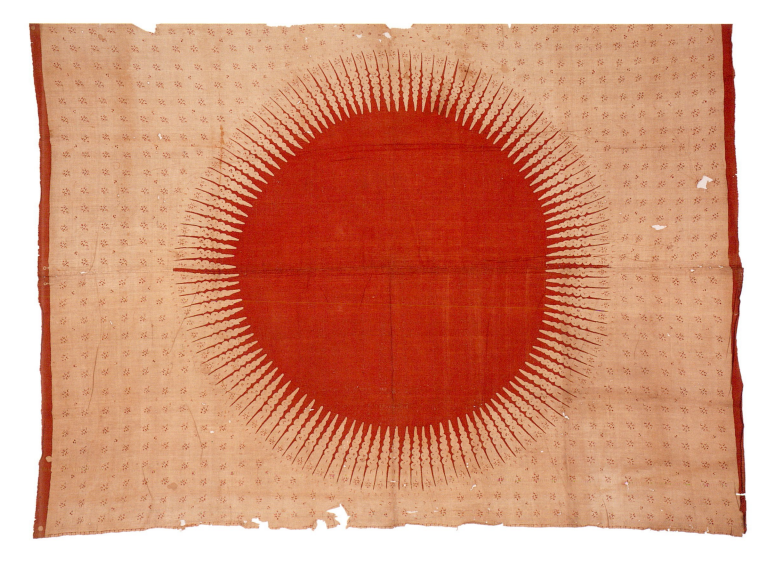

Coromandel coast, India
Traded to south Sumatra, Indonesia
Ceremonial cloth and sacred heirloom [*dodot*]   17th–18th century
handspun cotton, natural dyes, mordants; mordant painting
282.0 x 207.0 cm
Gift of Michael and Mary Abbott 1988
1988.1596

Gujarat, India
Traded to Sulawesi, Indonesia
Ceremonial cloth and sacred heirloom   17th–18th century (detail)
handspun cotton, natural dyes, mordants; mordant block printing, batik
365.0 x 92.5 cm
Conserved with the assistance of Isobel Williams
Gift of Michael and Mary Abbott 1988
1989.1333

Gujarat, India
Traded to Sulawesi, Indonesia
Ceremonial cloth and sacred heirloom 16th century (detail)
handspun cotton, natural dyes, mordants; mordant block printing, batik
492.0 x 91.0 cm
Conserved with the assistance of the Textiles Workshop,
Canberra School of Art, Australian National University
Gift of Michael and Mary Abbott 1988
1988.1626

Gujarat, India
Traded to Sulawesi, Indonesia
Ceremonial cloth and sacred heirloom   17th–18th
century (detail)
handspun cotton, natural dyes, mordants; mordant
block printing, mordant painting, batik
484.0 x 100.8 cm
Conserved with the assistance of Kate Williams
Gift of Michael and Mary Abbott 1988
1989.1334

India
Traded to Lampung, Sumatra, Indonesia
Ceremonial hanging [*sarasa* or *leluhur*]   17th–18th century
cotton, mordants; mordant painting and printing
Loan from the Collection of Robert J. Holmgren and Anita Spertus, New York

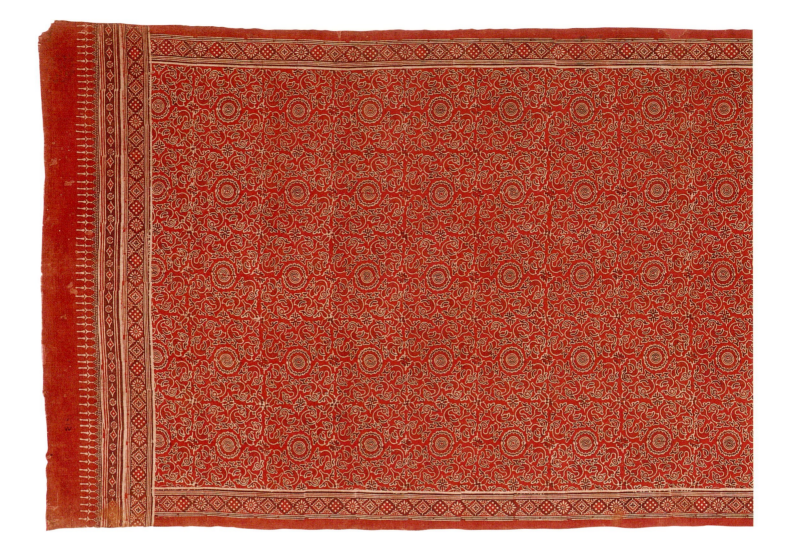

Gujarat, India
Traded to Sulawesi, Indonesia
Ceremonial cloth and sacred heirloom early 15th – early 17th century (detail)
cotton, natural dyes, mordants; mordant block printing, batik
110.0 x 553.5 cm
Conserved with the assistance of Diana Walder
Gift of Michael and Mary Abbott 1987
1987.1068

Gujarat, India
Traded to Toraja region, central Sulawesi, Indonesia
Ceremonial cloth and sacred heirloom [*mawa* or *ma'a*] 17th–18th century (detail)
cotton, natural dyes, natural mordants; mordant block printing, pigment painting, batik
91.5 x 418.0 cm
1983.3686

Gujarat, India
Traded to Toraja region, central Sulawesi, Indonesia
Ceremonial cloth and sacred heirloom [*ma'a*] 1500 (detail)
cotton, natural dyes, mordants; mordant painting, batik
102.0 x 534.0 cm
Conserved in loving memory of Edwin D. Alcott
Gift of Michael and Mary Abbott 1989
1989.1329

Gujarat, India
Traded to Toraja region, Sulawesi, Indonesia
Ceremonial cloth and sacred heirloom [*ma'a*]   17th century
cotton, natural dyes, mordants; mordant block printing, batik
107.0 x 500.0 cm
1984.3175

Gujarat, India
Traded to Toraja region, Sulawesi, Indonesia
Ceremonial cloth and sacred heirloom [*ma'a*]   15th–16th century (detail)
handspun cotton, natural dyes, mordants; mordant block printing, batik
94.0 x 439.0 cm
Gift of Michael and Mary Abbott 1987
1987.1069

Gujarat, India
Traded to Toraja region, Sulawesi, Indonesia
Ceremonial cloth and sacred heirloom [*ma'a*]   early 14th – early 15th century
handspun cotton, natural dyes, mordants; mordant block printing, batik
92.0 x 535.0 cm
Conserved with the assistance of Mrs Rosanna Hindmarsh
Gift of Michael and Mary Abbott 1988
1988.1625

Coromandel coast, India
Traded to Toraja region, Sulawesi, Indonesia
Ceremonial cloth and sacred heirloom [*ma'a*]
15th–16th century (detail)
handspun cotton, natural dyes, mordants; mordant
block printing, batik
90.0 x 484.0 cm
Gift of Michael and Mary Abbott 1991
1991.637

Deccan region, India
Traded to Belu region, Timor, Indonesia
Ceremonial cloth and sacred heirloom 17th–18th century (detail)
handspun cotton, natural dyes, mordants; mordant painting, batik
166.0 x 230.0 cm
Conserved with the assistance of the Maxwell Family in memory of Anthony Forge
1994.1456

(left) Masulipatam, Andhra Pradesh, India
Traded to Indonesia
Ceremonial cloth and sacred heirloom
late 19th century
handspun cotton, natural dyes, mordants;
mordant block printing, pigment painting
211.0 x 125.0 cm
Conserved with the assistance of
Esther Raworth
Gift of Michael and Mary Abbott 1988
1988.1623

(opposite) Coromandel coast, India
Traded to Bali, Indonesia
Heirloom hanging
late 17th century
cotton, natural dyes, mordants; mordant
painting
164.0 x 106.0 cm
Gift of Cecilia Ng in memory of Anthony Forge
2002.152

(above) Coromandel coast, India
Traded to Sulawesi, Indonesia
Ceremonial cloth and sacred heirloom 18th centruy (detail)
handspun cotton, natural dyes, mordants; mordant painting, batik
354.0 x 109.0 cm
Gift of Michael and Mary Abbott 1988
1989.1335

(opposite) Coromandel coast, India
Traded to eastern Indonesia
Ceremonial cloth and sacred heirloom 18th century (detail)
handspun cotton, natural dyes, mordants; mordant painting, batik, pigment painting
383.0 x 131.5 cm
Conserved with the assistance of Lyn Williams AM
1991.726

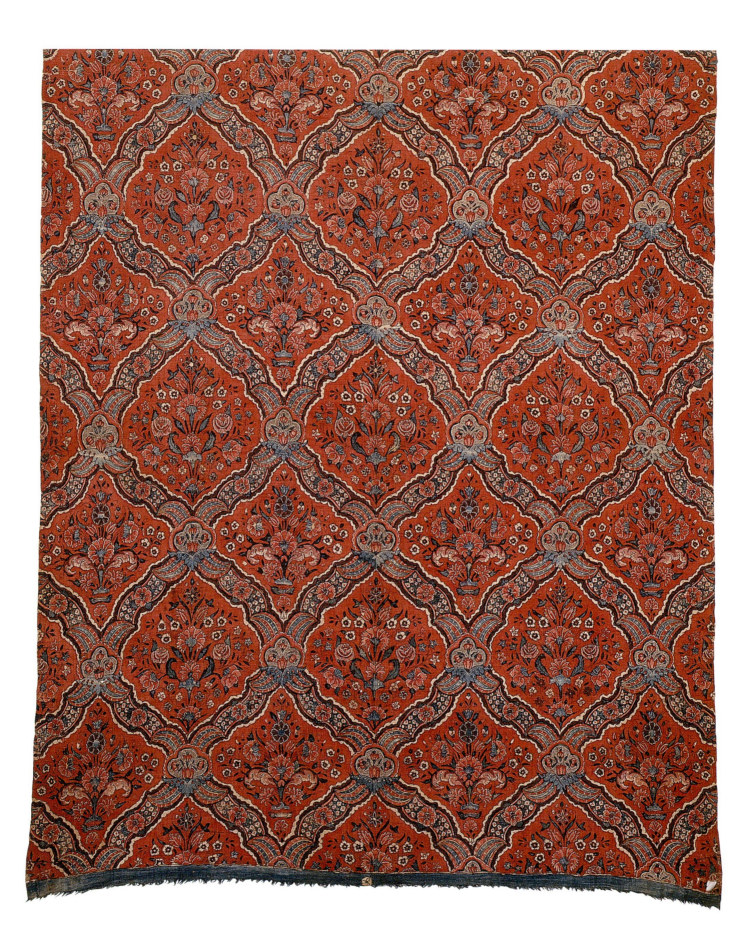

(above) Coromandel coast, India
Traded to Sulawesi, Indonesia
Ceremonial cloth and sacred heirloom [*ma'a*] 18th century
handspun cotton, natural dyes, mordants; mordant painting, batik
352.0 x 112.5 cm
Gift of Michael and Mary Abbott 1989
1989.1325

(opposite) Coromandel coast, India
Traded to Indonesia
Ceremonial cloth and sacred heirloom early 18th century (detail)
handspun cotton, natural dyes, mordants; mordant painting, batik
405.0 x 115.0 cm
Conserved with the assistance of Brian O'Keeffe AO and Bridget O'Keeffe AM
Gift of Michael and Mary Abbott 1988
1988.1612

Coromandel coast, India
Traded to Indonesia
Ceremonial cloth and sacred heirloom [*ma'a*]
early 18th century (detail)
handspun cotton, natural dyes, mordants; mordant
painting, batik
360.0 x 115.5 cm
Gift of Michael and Mary Abbott 1988
1988.1614

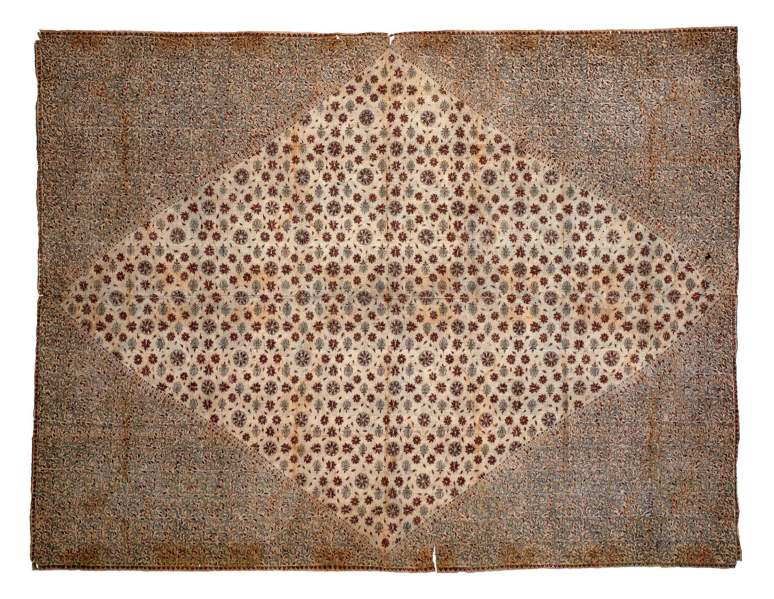

Coromandel coast, India
Traded to south Sumatra, Indonesia
Ceremonial cloth and sacred heirloom [*dodot*] 17th–18th century
cotton, natural dyes, mordants; block printing, mordant painting
210.0 x 275.0 cm
Gift of Michael and Mary Abbott 1987
1987.1071

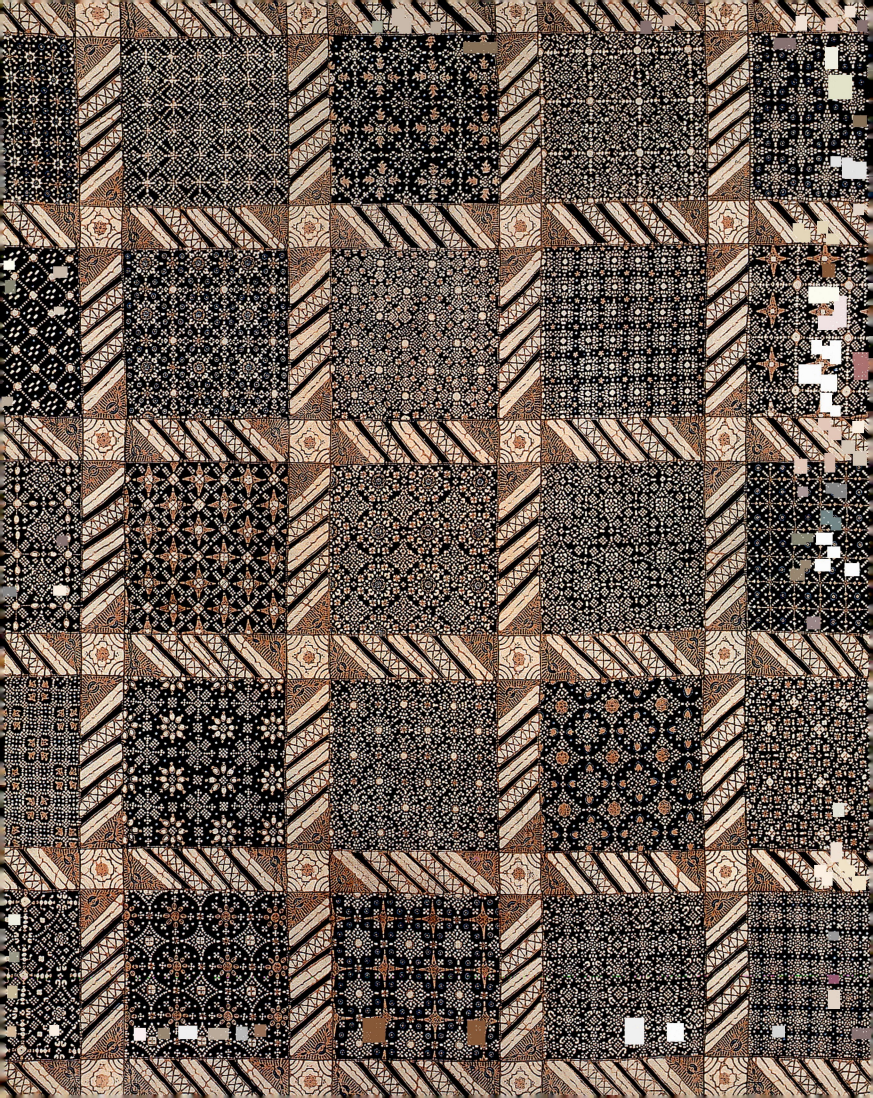

5 CREATIVE EXCHANGES
Indian textiles and Indonesian responses

Over centuries the trade in cloth stimulated the most animated and enduring conversations between India and Indonesia on textile design and form. The centrality of textiles in Indonesia for sacred rites and everyday clothing, and the strength and range of local textile skills provided a fertile environment for the absorption of exotic elements into the region's textile traditions. This centuries-old engagement with a surprisingly rich and constantly expanding source of design, motif, pattern and layout can be traced throughout textile producing centres across the entire archipelago. The considerable diversity in textile types, regional and local styles, and decorative techniques across Indonesia has meant that the 'Indian' elements were absorbed, adapted and transformed in an endless number of ways: while some weavers attempted to replicate the complete design from an exotic fabric, others translated a mere fragment of a motif into completely new interpretations. Ultimately it was not just the textiles but the designs and motifs that came to be treasured by Indonesians and, like the Indian cloths themselves, often owned and controlled by people of noble rank, prestige and power, the textile designs came to symbolise high status in their own right, often without conscious reference to the trade cloth sources.

The motivations for exchanges of Indian and Indonesian designs and motifs must also have been many and varied. So too were the creative responses that the interplay between Indian and Indonesian textiles evoked. To some extent an understanding of these transpositions can be found in the functions of local textiles displaying Indian trade cloth imagery. The fragility of ancient and valued textile heirlooms must

certainly have stimulated the desire to preserve the beauty, magic and meaning in the finest local products in many communities. Many of the locally painted cotton *mawa* of the Toraja peoples clearly draw on Indian counterparts and, over time, they too have been absorbed into the category of textiles of the East. Even the technique is foreign to the ancestral traditions of cloth creation.

One of the most unlikely yet widely appreciated Indian chintz designs to be integrated into Indonesian textile iconography was the colourful *palampore* flowering tree. It inspired the Toraja to create monochrome block-printed versions that were radically different from any other local Sulawesi textiles. The symbolism of the tree of life and the sacred mountain is shared by many cultures, including India and Indonesia. The universal appeal of the flowering tree found on Indian trade chintzes for both Eastern and Western markets was very wide and the attraction of the motif on cloths associated with the upper worlds and the heavens, as in the popular *lelangit* or *lelehur* canopies, resonated across groups of very different religious orientations. The *palampore* provided an equally fitting image of the Hindu-Buddhist wishing tree and of Islamic Paradise, strikingly ornamental and well suited for hangings. It was also a formidable symbol of the *axis mundi* that linked the abode of deified ancestors with the world of humans, its roots stretching down into watery lower realms.

It is not surprising then that the pervasive tree symbol of Indonesian art often follows the *palampore* form. However, it is only in rare instances, like the sacred *mawa* (*ma'a*) textiles associated by the Toraja with the ceremonies of the East, of life and fertility, of agriculture and marriage, of prosperity for community and family, that the Indian and local textiles function interchangeably. In most instances the image of the flowering tree is transformed to fit the textile format or the regional style, as it does on the brilliant, bold Sumatran gold-thread embroidered hangings of spreading trees on mirror mounds with giant birds or on the subtle silken bands of the Lampung women's *tapis* where the flowering branches dwarf the characteristic sinuous trunk. Elsewhere the material of sequins and spangles distracts attention from the motif itself. The Islamic potted conifer within a domed *mihrab* niche has had much less appeal, although it may have inspired a number of motifs that resemble flowers and branches in vases and urns.

Across north-coast Java, however, the ornamental qualities of the tree design are manipulated in marvellous ways, and the chintz-like quality achieved by exquisite hand-drawn batik on European superfine milled cotton more than surpassed the Indian prototypes in popularity both throughout the Indonesian littoral and beyond. It was the charming variations on the multi-floral design — and it was a design that permitted, in fact actually encouraged, elaboration and experimentation — that established Javanese batik as the cloth of choice not only in Sumatra and Bali, but also in Malaysia and Cambodia, and even as far a field as Japan.

The intersection between landscape scenes and flowering tree designs is a feature of both Indian mordant-painted and Javanese batik textiles. In Java the diminution of the tree and the repetition of the mountains to form landscape imagery became particularly pronounced on fabric for royal garments. That this coincided with the burgeoning of Javanese batik techniques in the 18th and 19th centuries is suggested by the survival of Indian textiles in Indonesian style and royal *dodot* wrap form, and by the appearance of the landscape scenes on some of the earliest extant batiks hand-drawn on locally spun cotton cloth, also in formats of courtly apparel. In one early Cirebon landscape the layered rocks and grottoes are inhabited not by composite animals but by the mermaid archer Dewi Urang Ayu, daughter of a powerful sea god and a wife of one of the key *Mahabharata* heroes, Bima. However, the association of the landscape motifs in gold-leaf techniques also stretches back centuries, recorded on the *wayang* puppets and *wayang beber* scroll paintings of Java. Early 19th-century painted wooden models depicting Javanese aristocrats, collected by Sir Stamford Raffles during his short rule as English Governor of the East Indies, wear *dodot* decorated with landscape imagery apparently worked in gold leaf.

While the imagery remains similar, a fundamental shift in technique on Java — from mordant painting to batik resist — led to unexpected stylistic changes. North-coast batik makers successfully turned the batik process on its head, waxing out the entire background to leave the darker-coloured motifs sharp against the undyed white and faun — a far more difficult process than drawing the motif in mordants to take the colour, leaving the rest uncoloured. The batik makers of central

Java, however, pursued the logic of the batik technique, so that pale linear designs are created in wax resist to stand out against the dark browns and indigos of non-waxed backgrounds. Unlike their north-coast counterparts, these batik are dramatically different visually from the Indian originals.

Despite the inevitable change of palette, floral motifs adapted from Indian trade textiles take many forms. Many of the most popular batik textiles for export for Sumatra and Bali display simple floral forms interlaced with tendrils and arabesques; the stylised carnations, tulips and roses suggest that the many Mughal-inspired continuous patterns of this type were the source of inspiration.

It is not surprising that such rare, beautiful and highly valued objects as the Indian imported textiles should impress local Indonesian weavers. Their prestige and the sacred significance that time and religion had invested in them made them suitable sources for inspiration for local ceremonial textiles. In many cases, the prestige of locally made cloths bearing trade cloth designs is comparable with that awarded to the trade cloths themselves. The control traditional leaders and regional rulers had over the use of both the trade items and their local reproductions ensured this. Yet in Flores and the Solor archipelago, for instance, despite the similarity of the designs and motifs to Indian models, the warp ikat cloths are distinctively eastern Indonesian. The characteristic red-brown *Morinda citrifolia* dyes (locally known as *mengkudu*), the thick cotton base, the size and the artistic style are unmistakably the marks of local Indonesian genius.

It is not only the physical qualities of the Indonesian textiles that disguise their sources of inspiration. The translations of foreign images into Indonesian styles have led to some remarkable yet mysterious designs. None is perhaps more important yet more obscure than the developments of designs from an international set of luxury textile patterns that, while they appeared as early as the 15th century, were extremely popular in Europe in the early to mid-18th century. Often attributed to Italian origins, creative variations in expensive materials such as cut velvets and metallic brocades, damask and embroidery were favoured by the nobility of Europe and the Ottoman Empire. The designs were reproduced on Indian mordant-painted textiles, apparently for the international market in the early 18th century.

Their popularity in Indonesia led to considerable numbers being produced for that market, in increasingly crude versions as the brilliant pinks and blues of the earlier examples gave way to dull red-browns and blacks. The design, however, sparked a fluorescence of patterns that are now seen as quintessentially Indonesian. The vases and lamps, ribbons and lattices, drapes and swags gave way to luscious designs that increasingly lost any resemblance or reference to the originals. The gradual shift from European to Indonesian rococo is most clearly seen in the silk weft ikat shawls and sashes of south Sumatra and Bangka. The intricate jewel-like patterns, some of the finest examples of weft ikat decoration to have been created, are purely ornamental, as of course were the European and Islamic prototypes.

In central Java, where the Italianate designs also caught the attention of the nobility, a different aesthetic was at work. There the indigo blue and *soga* brown palettes of the palace batik combined with an enlargement and elongation of elements, sometimes transformed into pavilions and shrines, curving wings and sinuous snakes but also into enigmatic shapes that gave no clue to their origin and meaning. The resulting patterns included the enigmatic *pisang balik* and some of the more mysterious variants on *semen* designs, batik patterns restricted to royal use. While the name *semen* (from *semi*, sprout) indicates that these include foliage and forest images, the *pisang balik* (upside-down banana) or *pisang bali* (Balinese banana) do not. Rather, like many modern names for motifs, they indicate a literal interpretation of the form rather than the knowledge of a motif's pedigree. The exclusivity of the designs, however, is firmly routed in a history of the control of luxury trade items. Hence these patterns, like others derived from Indian treasures, are worn only by members of the Javanese aristocracy. In the central principalities in particular, it was the silk *patola* that had been conspicuously worn in the royal court — as skirts and sashes by princes and princesses alike. The same applied to locally made batik exhibiting trade cloth patterns.

While the *sari*-length *patola* was occasionally tailored into pants for the Javanese nobility, the valuable lengths were rarely cut. For some markets — notably Bali and south Sumatra — small versions of the *patola* were made specifically for trade. These were narrower and shorter, similar in dimension to local sashes, shoulder and breast-cloths and, judging by the transposition of their patterns onto local silks, ultimately interchangeable. In fact the local versions were usually much more tightly woven and more finely ikat dyed than the small export *patola*.

The recent appearance in Indonesia of certain forms of historical Indian trade textiles has raised questions about the relationship between market demands and export production. It has long been recognised that the 5-metre *sari* lengths of the Gujarat *patola* were generally unsuitable as Indonesian garments; there, the preferred skirtcloth length was at best only half of those dimensions, and often less. While we know little of contemporary use, in those cultures where very old trade textiles have survived they have rarely been used as clothing but rather as ritual objects.

Yet while in many cases the trade treasures were not worn, their prestigious patterns were dyed and woven into local garments especially for and by members of the elite, connecting the personal display with the ownership and control of exotic items of wealth. That many of the batik designs drawn directly or even obscurely from *patola* and chintzes belong to the repertoire of forbidden designs, exclusively worn by the rulers of the central Javanese principalities, reflects the prestige of the Indian motifs. In Lembata, however, the communal ownership of specific Indian heirloom textiles is reflected in warp ikat motifs: a clan's specific *patola* design is adopted in heraldic central fields on the ceremonial skirts of its female kin for bride wealth exchange and costume. In fact the women's skirt may preserve the memory of *patola* ownership now relinquished.

In Lembata, and throughout the entire archipelago, the most popular family of motifs is arguably adapted from *patola* with geometric patterned fields. In particular the round eight-pointed star within a square grid appears across the entire Indonesian archipelago — in hand spun cottons, in flimsy silks, in batik and gold leaf.

In some instances it is not only the field pattern that has been inspired by Indian double ikats. Elements of border bands and triangular ends have also been incorporated into Indonesian textiles. Nowhere is this more pronounced than in central Flores where the ceremonial shawls worn by the clan leaders emulate very closely their *patola* predecessors, although in single warp rather than double ikat. Even the choice of colours mirrors the original, although the deep, saturated red-brown cotton lacks the brilliance of the brighter silks. In central Java, where overall patterning is preferred, the glow of the silks is achieved by calendering and gliding the surface of the sombre cotton batik.

While the influence of star *patola* on Indonesian design has been long recognised by local weavers and art historians, the heritage of other recurring patterns was less clear. Certainly Indian block-printed textiles with *patola*-like layout hinted at the possibility of other Indonesian motifs having *patola* origins. The presence of one widely recurring pattern on many very special textiles — on the rare Iban *pua sungkit*, created as the name suggests like *songket*, with supplementary threads (although wrapped around the warp threads rather than floating over them), on the Balinese double ikat *geringsing*, on south Sumatran weft ikat sashes, on Lio men's warp ikat shawls and on batik. Its presence on the weft ikat *kain cepuk* of Bali and the central panels of many ceremonial skirts from south Lembata sent clear signals of *patola* origins. Both these categories of cloth appear to serve as memory banks for past heirlooms now lost or in precarious state. The format of *kain cepuk*, whether in cotton or in silk, also follows very closely the layout of the Indian *patola*, with field motifs mirroring the double ikat. The patterns on the Lembata skirts, so essential for elaborate exchanges that cement the bonds between families at weddings and funerals, draw directly on the family's treasured *patola*, stored in clan temples. As the sacred treasures become fragile or disappear, the inventory of *patola* patterns appears to have been gradually transferred onto sturdy and renewable local cloth.

The existence in the past of a considerably wider range of designs on the *patola* double ikat traded to Indonesia has recently been proven. The recent appearance of 'lost' *patola*, especially in the Lampung region, has thrown considerable light on these designs and confirmed previous suppositions by art historians that certain types of designs, widespread in Indonesia and found on local textiles where *patola*-derived patterns are often displayed, were indeed the legacy of *patola* that had long since disappeared. It is also now evident that while some of these *patola* designs did survive on Indian cotton counterparts, locally made Indonesian textiles may provide the key to unlocking the historical repertoire of *patola* for trade. Yet the lack of Indian domestic evidence, and the fact that many of the recently discovered textiles are not in *sari* form, or in the tight weave demanded of Indian patrons but in the small export size, also raises questions about the original sources of some of these designs. The multiplicity of designs found in the central fields of south Sumatran *kain limar*, for example, may also have been inspired by cotton cloths of similar layout but for which there are no *patola* counterparts, as was clearly the case with Javanese batik.

The development of batik seems more intimately connected with Indian chintz rather than *patola*. The hand-drawn motifs on fine cotton often emulate the Indian patterns and motifs on textiles of proportions far better suited to Indonesian fashion, a shift from *sari* to *sarong* dimensions. In fact the growth of batik largely coincided with the demise of the Indonesian market for Indian cloth — brought on perhaps by shifts in the world economy and the replacement of the spices of old by new plantation crops, and by the closing of traditional markets in the face of competition from industrial Europe. For the burgeoning batik industry this meant a ready supply of fine milled cotton cloth, and eventually a ready supply of chemical dyes. That these were embraced by the commercial ateliers of the north coast rather than the palace workshops of the central domain mirrored the division between the two realms of batik production, which widened as time passed.

Since it was these Indian textiles that stimulated the growth of the local batik industry in Java, it is not surprising that, over time, popular designs appeared on both Indian trade cloth and Indonesian commercial batik. Indeed a vigorous exchange and appropriation of Indonesian and Indian patterns appears to have occurred on each side of the Bay of Bengal, although the techniques for producing the fabrics remained different: Javanese cottons were produced solely by wax resist batik where patterns, painted in molten wax onto the cloth's surface, were protected when the cloth was immersed in dye vats, in effect the direct opposite to the Indian mordant process. Like its Indian counterpart, it has been the Javanese batik industry of all Indonesian textile traditions that was the most easily able to respond to market demands and fashion changes: textiles were produced in regional Javanese styles for local Chinese and Arab communities and for export to neighbouring islands such as Bali where batik was never made.

While the palace guarded the exclusivity of fine batik, elsewhere in Java it became a key item of trade, its influence spreading like its Indian predecessors into the corners of the Indonesian archipelago and out into the wider Asian region. The styles that developed in batik also illuminated the dichotomy between palace and bazaar. North-coast batik continued to emulate Indian designs with bright designs on lighter backgrounds. In the interior kingdoms the sombre dark browns and indigos formed a regal background on which floated enigmatic references to nobility and high status, such as stylised Garuda wings and serpent coils, schematic landscapes and lotus ponds, and an overwhelming number of patterns that allude to expensive trade textiles. Only in the sultanates of north-coast Cirebon did India meet Indonesia in the bold imagery of fragrant gardens and rocky grottoes inhabited by mythical composite beasts.

Animals rarely feature as a major set of motifs in most textile producing areas in Indonesia, possibly because many textiles are created as functional garments even when they form a crucial part of marriage and other exchanges. It is thus not surprising that relatively few Indian textiles for the Indonesian market were dominated by motifs of animals, real or mythical. Narrative designs, however, do include animals that have proved popular in Indonesian art, though less in textiles: the processions and hunting scenes on Indian textiles depicting elephants, horses and camels only rarely appear to have had an impact on local textiles. The animated landscapes of Mughal art, with creatures battling each other amid flowers and foliage, were rarely emulated — although the rocks and mounds of some north-coast batik designs sometimes formed obscure mythical creatures.

The animal characters of epics and legends had great appeal to Indonesian artists although again largely in media other than textiles: the monkeys of the *Ramayana*, the mythical composite creatures of Hindu and Buddhist iconography with elephant trunk and lion body, and the winged Bouraq — half human, half horse and said to have transported the Prophet Muhammad to heaven — are sometimes pictured in the fluid techniques of batik and embroidery.

Yet it was one group of woven *patola* that appears to have most inspired the textile makers of Indonesia to incorporate animal motifs. Usually displaying elephant motifs, occasionally in a square grid with tigers, but at their most powerful and appealing in a huge series across sari-size textiles, this category of double ikats was made in Gujarat specifically for the Indonesian customers. What had once been a small border motif from the *patola* for the Indian domestic market now dominated the central field on export products, with single images and sometimes entire scenes of caparisoned elephants with mahouts, nobleman in howdahs, attendants with parasols and standards, and tigers and camels contained within diamond trellises. Subtle variations between designs can be discovered in small details such as the patterns on the elephant cloth, the parrots floating above and the sprigs of flowers underfoot — all devices reworked from the same domestic border patterns. More markedly there are dramatically different combinations of red and black backgrounds. While the *Art of the Patola*, the 1979 two-volume landmark study by Alfred Bühler and Eberhard Fisher, registered only six extant examples, dozens have since come to light, evidence of the popularity of the great elephant *patola* throughout the archipelago. It has now been established that the large elephant motif was replicated on cloths of the small export dimensions, with concomitant Indonesian features appearing only in those designs. In particular the simplified forms include human figures with stylised *wayang*-style coiffeur on and inside the elephants.

The aesthetic preferences of each regional textile culture, the techniques with which the designs are reproduced, and the function of the object being created have led to a wealth of variants in the transpositions and translations of the *patola* elephant motifs onto Indonesian textiles. In Bali designs follow the Indian prototypes in many ways, appearing on silk garments for aristocratic men and women in colours similar to the originals. In eastern Indonesia, however, where the weavers captured the status symbols in the sombre indigo hues, the transfigurations are enigmatic: the stick-figure creatures with long trunks interspersed with diamond lozenges have made a long journey into the vocabulary of the most prestigious textiles of the Nggada and Endeh regions of central Flores. Any doubt is dispelled by the name of the motif, *nggaja* — a variation on the Sanskrit-based pan-Indonesian word *gajah* for the royal symbol, the elephant. Since the elephant *patola* are now known to have been popular heirlooms in Lampung also, the elephant figures on many of that region's textiles may also have been modelled on the Indian *patola* version.

There were numerous other techniques and patterns that appealed to Indonesian textile makers and consumers over the centuries. Many suggest a long period of interaction and exchange between the Indian sub-continent and the islands of Indonesia. The popularity of checks and plaids, especially throughout Islamic Indonesia, may stem from early imports of bales of simpler patterns. The generic Indonesian term for this form of plaid textiles, *pelekat*, reflects early Indian connections, derived apparently from the town of Pulicat on the Coromandel coast. In this way it mirrors *madras*, the international term for checked cotton cloth, which takes its name from the Indian trading port Madras further to the south. The English term for the plain-woven calico follows the same pattern, from the Indian port city of Calicut. The ubiquitous cylindrical check *sarong* is found everywhere across the islands, and has been especially identified with seagoing communities such as the Buginese of Sulawesi. In many regions, ceremonial dress follows the same styles and patterns, with fine silk plaids replacing the sturdier everyday cottons. The commercial success of these maritime trading communities in purveying locally made check *sarong* throughout the region is a further example of Indonesia textile production capturing the local and wider Asian market with a form modified to better suit local tastes.

Other decorative techniques found on Indian trade textiles destined for the Indonesian islands include metallic and supplementary thread brocades, embroidery and mirror-work. There is also stylistic evidence for trade in tie-dyed cloth. Woven cloth decorated with tie-dye resist patterning has not generally been highly valued in Indonesia. Unlike batik, the technique has never reached its zenith in any culture in the archipelago, and tie-dyed cloths have tended to be used as attractive ornamental accessories rather than textiles crucial to ritual activities. While it is possible that the finely dyed *bandani* shawls from Rajasthan in west India did reach the islands of Indonesia, there is more evidence that cotton textiles imitating the spotted tie-dye technique through hand-drawn or block-printed methods were imported from India.

Whether the huge bold mordant-painted and batik-decorated *mawa* (or *ma'a*) hanging long stored in the Toraja region of Sulawesi was a source of inspiration for the Toraja people's own bold tie-dyed *roto* textiles or whether the Indian textiles were made in *roto* designs is unknown. The function and meaning of the *roto* themselves is shrouded in mystery although they may well have filled the same roles as the Indian cotton *mawa* in the festivals of prosperity and life.

In Sumatra and Bali the soft tie-dyed Chinese silk sashes and breastcloths are bright accessories to formal dress. Like the *roto*, the asymmetrical patterning on resist dyed textiles from Bali and Lombok seems to have been peculiar to this technique. In contrast, the shoulder cloths of Palembang with their *boteh* cone end borders do have an Indian resonance, although this may well be due to the 19th-century international fashion craze for Kashmir and later Paisley shawls rather than any direct Indian connections.

On Java, however, the diagonal orientation of many of the designs and the presence of the central lozenge links them to other aristocratic textiles such as the *dodot* and *kemben*. Unlike the status-laden batik, the stitch-decorated breast-cloths and *dodot* are associated with significant rites of passage suggesting a more ancient indigenous heritage. Reflecting their position as a more ancient form of textile, the flowered cloth (*kembangan*) as they are known remain an essential part of the annual offerings of the Sunan of Surakarta to the goddess of the South Seas, his spiritual bride.

The relationship between Indian textiles and the Indonesian market was undoubtedly complex. The wide appreciation of many exotic designs is evident in the range of surviving Indian fabrics. It is also reflected in the adoption of key motifs and designs from those sources into Indonesian textile vocabularies. One family of patterns could be viewed as a summation of Indian and Indonesian textile intersections and is particularly illuminating in terms of both its role as a repository of the patterns of Indian textiles from the past and of the ways in which batik makers have adapted the motifs to local taste. Checked, striped and zigzag patterns continue to be very popular across central and western Indonesia, particularly in pattern-woven techniques such as plaid and *songket* brocade. However, it is the graphic potential of hand-drawn batik that has captured the essence of many of the Indian patterns, in form if not in colour.

The arrangement and enclosure of designs in diagonal stripes and zigzagging chevrons exudes a very Indonesian flavour, and rare surviving Indian trade cottons in these formats appear to be made exclusively for the Indonesian market. The diagonal bands of the *parang rusak* (broken sword) design are viewed by many as the most quintessential symbol of the Javanese court and by extrapolation of Java itself. In contrast, the use of zigzag patterning today is almost exclusively associated with north-coast principalities and with the delicate batiks of the mestizo Chinese communities. While in central Java the patchwork (*tambal*) design is exclusively worn by young aristocratic women in particular court rituals, outside the palace circles similar designs are encountered on north-coast and other Javanese regional styles.

The patchwork layout, however, has much more ancient ancestry: its symbolism lies in the Buddhist practice of eschewing earthly luxury to pursue a life of mendicant poverty. The simple apparel of such seekers of truth comprises cloth cobbled together from scraps. Rulers and high-ranking clergy alike have long manipulated this custom to create robes and cloaks from carefully chosen swatches of the finest brocade. Javanese rulers were no exception, and 19th-century versions of the royal talismanic jacket, *kotang antakusuma*, were created from a patchwork of shimmering imported brocades and velvets. Like many

aspects of Javanese culture, the legendary power of the *antakusuma* drew on many traditions. It was said to have originally been created from the skin of Ananta, the great serpent of Indic mythology, yet Sunan Kalijaga, one of the nine mystical saints attributed with spreading Islam through Java, is also credited with making the first *antakusuma* and it is annually venerated by his descendants and followers. However, the *kotang antakusuma* was also one of the attributes of the demi-god Gatotkaca, allowing him to fly. The practice of wearing batik tunics and skirtcloths created by patching remained evident in the culture of the remote mountain people of Tengger in central Java who practised a form of mystical Hinduism until very recent times.

In each of these formats it is the content of the designs that draw on other textile patterns that is among the most fascinating. A patchwork from the Jogjakarta court will, for example, incorporate triangles of other batik patterns including the *parang rusak* diagonal stripes. These sometimes alternate with noble or auspicious creatures and objects such as crowned *naga*, Garuda wings, elephants and lotuses. On one level the *tambal* designs might be viewed as an encyclopaedia of the prestigious courtly patterns of the time. However, the older versions of the patchwork batik are filled with designs that relate more closely to Indian trade cloth than local batik patterns, again sequestering the highest status textile patterns available for court use. The palette of blues and reds on white backgrounds also mirrored the aesthetic of Indian chintz. We have already seen that many of the most popular batik patterns are themselves stylised versions of the Indian prototypes: in fact as more old Indian trade textiles come to light, the more closely this vocabulary is seen to be aligned.

A linear history of the interplay between India and Indonesia, however, is complicated by the readiness of Indian textile makers to satisfy their customers. Thus we find Indian textiles in forms such as the huge royal *dodot* wraps, only marketable in certain parts of the archipelago and with particular noble clientele. Once a popular Indonesia format had been reached — at whose instigation is an unknown — a large proportion of the export trade from India was couched in that design layout. Floral and geometric motifs, birds and animals, lozenges and roundels, and lattices and arabesques were similarly realigned and crafted into suitable patterns to fill the central field of the *sembagi* and *sarasa*, approximately 2.5-metre-long lengths and up to a metre wide, framed by narrow borders and embellished with triangular teeth across each end. Indian textiles were shipped in lengths to be cut into this popular *sarong* length; batik textiles were made to measure to the same design. This format has dominated Indonesian textiles for centuries. It is the design of the south Sumatran shoulder cloths, sashes and skirts for men and women. It is reflected in the ceremonial shawls of the clan leaders of central Flores, and in the sacred dance sash of the Balinese witch Rangda. It is draped around the body or sewn into cylinders to form decorative head panels where the points of the triangles meet. The design structure was applied to embroideries and batik, to gold brocade and silk weft ikat.

The interplay between source and transformation and of prototypes and translations continues to unfold. So the appearance, in south Sumatra, of a number of small embroidered samplers with details of motifs and fragments of continuous patterns that relate very closely to those found on south Sumatran *songket* brocade is mysterious. The use of samplers is unusual in Indonesian textile production. A woman may pore over a fine old example of an important textile type, examining the proportions of the motifs and the combinations of colours, but the use of pattern guides in any textile technique is very rare. The form of stitching and the patterns on these recently discovered samplers appear closely related to the south Indian *kalasthi* embroidery styles used to decorate the *sari* but which have been largely extinct for the past century. However, many of the motifs and the fragments of continuous patterns and sample borders have surprising parallels in the embroideries and samplers of other parts of the Islamic world: the similarities in birds, stylised trees, geometric meanders and S-spirals between, for example, medieval Egypt and south Sumatra may be evidence of the strength of international maritime conversations stretching back into an uncharted past. On the other hand they may reflect the constrictions of certain techniques or the propensity of humans to create parallel attractive shapes. In south Sumatra, however, the images on the needlework samplers bear less relationship to local embroideries than to popular brocade designs. Found in the hinterland of the port city of Palembang, their appearance may reflect a symbiotic relationship between capital and region, between court and village. Women in the hinterland may have woven fine textiles for the centre, with orders placed according to the patterns on the samplers. These pattern include suggestions for many variations on triangular borders, on birds and flowers, on gryphons and dragons, and even for inscriptions in Arabic and Roman lettering.

The spread of Indian-inspired textile motifs in some regions may reflect the relationship between the courts and their realm. While a royal court may have controlled much of the wealth in Indian cloth, its economic wellbeing depended on produce from its region. If the passage of certain prestige Indian textiles into the hinterland was, for political or economic reasons, controlled or abandoned, the development of charming and visually similar local counterparts created in traditional Indonesian techniques for vital exchange may have been the impetus for the transfer of designs and patterns onto local cloths both in the coastal courts and in the interior domains.

It is not only in the structure and form of the textile that questions of origin arise. Some unusual motifs found on both Indian chintz and on local Indonesian textiles are particularly problematic. The distinctive patterns achieved in double ikat resist on certain Balinese *geringsing* textiles very mysteriously appear on Indian chintz *dodot* in Lampung, the pattern hand-drawn in mordants filling the central diamond-shaped field of the large textiles. The mandala shape and the small steeped blocks of purple-brown clearly imitate a woven prototype. Yet whether this pattern has its origins in the brooding sombre hues of the Balinese *geringsing*, possibly in the past presenting a more dramatically contrasting pattern, is uncertain. A small group of very finely patterned weft ikat textiles has also come to light recently in Lampung; of considerable age, they appear stylistically and technically to have been locally patterned in weft ikat, although the presence of woven gold bands across the plain end borders is reminiscent of the *pallav* of an Indian *sari*. Their characteristic *geringsing* designs suggest that, while today this is confined to Bali, the motifs may once have enjoyed a wider appreciation. Of course, acknowledging the presence of *patola* patterns on Balinese *geringsing* and south Sumatran *kain limar*, there is also the possibility that this too could be a lost *patola* design.

The avenues for exchange between India and Indonesia have long been broken, a casualty of the modern era with its less porous national boundaries and the diminution of international sea trade. At both ends of this ancient conduit, however, textile traditions continued to be rich and vibrant. Both India and Indonesia have continued to offer much to international textile designers and artists.

The changes in the social and economic structure of both India and Indonesia have had profound effects on textile symbolism: a more egalitarian approach has seen once-forbidden patterns used by many. The luxury fabrics once beyond the reach of all but a small elite can now be hired for weddings by those with the interest and the wherewithal. The dispensation that had sometimes existed in the past to couples who, as king and queen for their wedding day, were permitted to don luxury apparel normally reserved for the aristocracy is no longer required. In fact the survival of certain prestige textiles is no longer in the hands of aristocratic patrons but in those who admire the skills and beauty of fine handmade textiles that reveal the traditions of the past.

In Indonesia, as has long been the case in India, the commercial market for traditional textiles has seen design and production shift to men in many instances. While this has been less obvious where older apparatus and techniques continue to be used, the introduction of new technologies has usually heralded a gender shift in the cultural symbolism of cloth and allowed men to move comfortably into textile production. Batik has been particularly open to this with men among the best-known designers for batik. The introduction of the metal stamp (*cap*) in the mid-19th century to counteract the importation of cheaply produced factory-printed textiles with designs closely emulating those of batik was perhaps a turning point. While women continued to create hand-drawn batik resists using the pen-like *canting*, from its inception *cap* batik-making has exclusively been the realm of men.

While fine textiles are still admired and artists strive to create items of refinement and great beauty, often drawing upon motifs and symbols from earlier religious beliefs and forms of cultural orientation, contemporary meanings focus on textiles as fine art and high fashion. The glamour and prestige of owning and wearing the finest hand-made textiles has not been lost. Yet after a century of rapid modernisation, with the spread of mass communications and universal education, the magical and sacred qualities of the finest textiles have everywhere receded. With their centrality in ceremonies of state and rites of passage largely dissipated, the need for treasuries of exotic cloth and the pressure to create and recreate exquisite local textiles has largely melted away. The survival of ancient designs in Indian and Indonesian textiles is now more archival than symbolic and the preservation of the objects and the skills a matter of heritage and history as much as of cultural meaning. Together these historical textiles provide vital clues to the spectacular textile traditions of India and Indonesia and to the intensity and endurance of the symbols and imagery of more than 500 years of exchange.

Further readings
Barnes, R, *The Ikat Textiles of Lamalera*, E.J. Brill, Leiden, 1989.
Bühler, A, & E Fischer, *The Patola of Gujarat*, 2 vols, Krebs AG, Basel, 1979.
Forge, A, 'Batik Patterns in the Early Nineteenth Century', in Gittinger, M (ed.), *To Speak With Cloth: Studies in Indonesian Textiles*, Fowler Museum for Cultural History, UCLA, Los Angeles, 1987.
Holmgren, RJ, & AE Spertus, *Early Indonesian Textiles from Three Island Cultures, Sumba-Toraja-Lampung*, Metropolitan Museum of Art, New York, 1989.
Holmgren, RJ, & AE Spertus, 'Is Geringsing Really Balinese?', in Völger, G, & K von Welck (eds), *Indonesian Textiles*, Ethnologica, Cologne, 1991.
Holmgren, RJ, & AE Spertus, 'Newly Discovered Patolu Motif Types — Extensions to Alfred Bühler and Eberhard Fischer (1979), The Patola of Gujarat', in Völger, G, & K von Welck (eds), *Indonesian Textiles*, Ethnologica, Cologne, 1991.
Maxwell, R, 'The Tree of Life in Indonesian Textiles: Ancient Iconography or Imported Chinoiserie?', in Völger, G, & K von Welck (eds), *Indonesian Textiles*, Ethnologica, Cologne, 1991.
Maxwell, R, *Textiles of Southeast Asia: Tradition, Trade and Transformation*, revised edition, Periplus, Singapore, 2003.
Nabholz-Kartaschoff, M, 'A Sacred Cloth of Rangda: Kain Cepuk of Bali and Nusa Penida', in Gittinger, M (ed.), *To Speak with Cloth: Studies in Indonesian Textiles*, Fowler Museum for Cultural History, UCLA, Los Angeles, 1987.

(opposite above) Gujarat, India
Traded to Indonesia
Ceremonial cloth and sacred heirloom [*patola*] 18th century (detail)
silk, natural dyes; double ikat
110.0 x 399.0 cm
Loan from the Collection of Robert J. Holmgren and Anita Spertus, New York

(opposite below) Gujarat, India
Traded to Lamahalot region, Solor or Lembata, Indonesia
Ceremonial cloth and sacred heirloom [*patola*] 18th century
silk, natural dyes; double ikat
113.0 x 510.0 cm
1984.3184

(above) Balinese people
Bali, Indonesia
Ceremonial breast cloth [*kamben endek*]   early 20th century
silk, dyes; weft ikat
61.5 x 352.0 cm
Conserved with the assistance of Ann Proctor
1989.1860

(right) Gujarat, India
Traded to Sumatra, Indonesia
Ceremonial cloth and sacred heirloom [*patola*]   18th century
silk, natural dyes; double ikat
260.0 x 86.0 cm
Conserved with the assistance of Lyn Conybeare and Christopher Conybeare AO
1991.1095

Coromandel coast, India
Traded to Sumatra, Indonesia
Ceremonial textile [*sarasa*]
17th–18th century
cotton, dyes, mordants; mordant painting
340.0 x 240.0 cm
Loan from the Collection of Robert J. Holmgren
and Anita Spertus, New York

Rongkong district, Sulawesi, Indonesia
Ceremonial hanging and shroud [*pori situtu*] c. 1910
cotton, dyes; warp ikat
167.0 x 298.0 cm
Acquired through gift and purchase
from the Collection of Robert J. Holmgren
and Anita Spertus, New York, 2000
2000.677

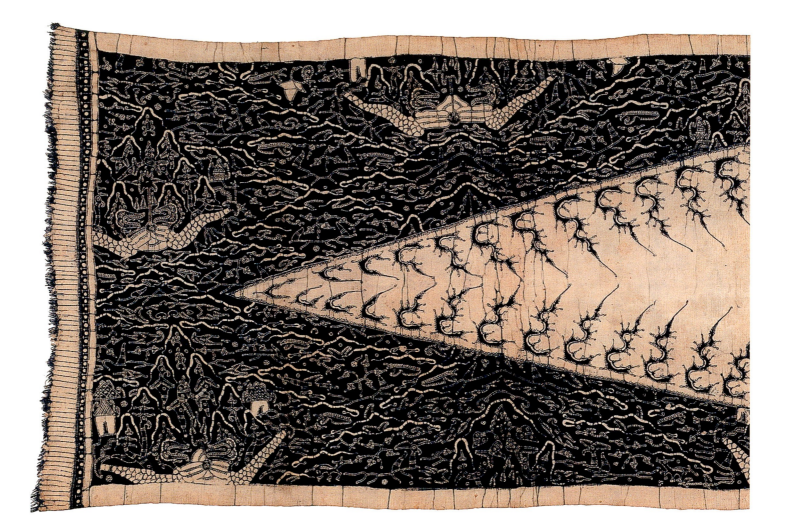

Cirebon, Java, Indonesia
Breast cloth [*kemben batik*]   19th century
cotton, dyes; hand-drawn batik
56.0 x 228.0 cm
Acquired through gift and purchase from the Collection of
Robert J. Holmgren and Anita Spertus, New York, 2000
2000.982

Gujarat, India
Traded to Sumatra, Indonesia
Patola 17th–18th century
silk, natural dyes; double ikat
244.0 x 91.0 cm
Loan from the Collection of Robert J. Holmgren and Anita Spertus, New York

Iban people
Sarawak, Malaysia
Ceremonial cloth [*pua sungkit*]   19th century
handspun cotton, natural dyes; supplementary weft
wrapping
182.0 x 103.0 cm
1981.1100

Iban people
Sarawak, Malaysia
Ceremonial cloth [*pua sungkit*]   19th century
handspun cotton, natural dyes; supplementary weft wrapping
209.0 x 94.0 cm
1982.2304

Sumbanese people
East Sumba, Indonesia
Man's cloth [*hinggi kombu*]   early 20th century
cotton, natural dyes; warp ikat, weft twining, staining
304.0 x 127.0 cm
1984.1240

Sumbanese people
Kanatang domain, Sumba, Indonesia
Man's cloth [*hinggi kombu*]   early 20th century
cotton, dyes; warp ikat, band weaving
249.0 x 93.0 cm
Conserved with the assistance of Sam Dixon
Acquired through gift and purchase from the Collection of
Robert J. Holmgren and Anita Spertus, New York, 2000
2000.990

Flores, Indonesia
Man's ceremonial shoulder cloth [*luka semba*] c. 1950
cotton, natural dyes; warp ikat
209.0 x 72.2 cm
1981.1142

Lamaholot people
Lembata, Indonesia
Woman's ceremonial skirt [*petak haren* or *kwatek nai telo*] 19th century
cotton, natural dyes; warp ikat
167.0 x 72.0 cm
1984.1219

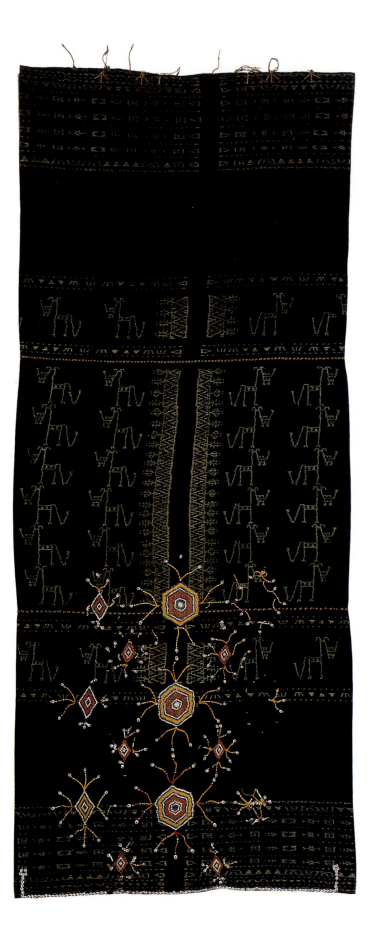

Ngada people
Bajawa district, Flores, Indonesia
Woman's ceremonial skirt [*lawo butu*]   19th century
handspun cotton, natural dyes, shells, beads; warp ikat, beading
185.0 x 79.0 cm
1981.1157

Maloh people
West Kalimantan, Indonesia
Woman's ceremonial jacket and skirt [*sape manik* and *kain manik*]
early 20th century
cotton, glass beads, shells, sequins; beading, appliqué
jacket 48.5 x 41.5 cm
skirt 58.0 x 42.0 cm
1985.1694

Java/Aceh, Indonesia
Woman's tunic [*baju kurung*]   late 19th century
cotton, natural dyes; hand-drawn batik
153.0 x 106.0 cm
1987.1818

Malay people
Jambi region, east Sumatra, Indonesia
Man's headcloth [*ikat kepala*]   late 19th century
cotton, natural dyes; hand-drawn batik
92.0 x 93.0 cm
Gift of Thomas Murray 2003
2003.223

Malay people
Palembang region, south Sumatra, Indonesia
Woman's ceremonial tunic [*baju kurung*]   late 19th – early 20th century
velvet, silk, sequins, gold thread; embroidery, couching
95.0 x 133.0 cm
1989.1865

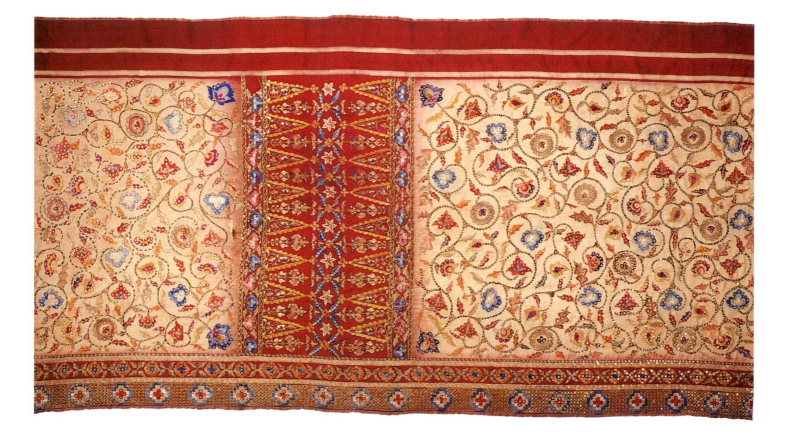

(above) West Kalimantan, Indonesia
Ceremonial skirt cloth [*kain kerlip*] 19th century
silk, sequins, gold thread; embroidery, appliqué, dip dyeing
100.2 x 185.3 cm
Conserved with the assistance of Dame Elisabeth Murdoch AC DBE
Acquired through gift and purchase from the Collection of
Robert J. Holmgren and Anita Spertus, New York, 2000
2000.780

(below) Palembang region, south Sumatra, Indonesia
Ceremonial hanging [*tirai*] 19th century
cotton, wool, gold thread, lead-backed, mirrors, beads;
couching, embroidery, appliqué
60.5 x 88.5 cm
1984.2001

Paminggir people
Lampung, south Sumatra, Indonesia
Ceremonial textile [*tampan*]   19th century
handspun cotton, dyes; supplementary weft weave
85.0 x 73.0 cm
Acquired through gift and purchase from the Collection of
Robert J. Holmgren and Anita Spertus, New York, 2000
2000.765

Paminggir people
Lampung, south Sumatra, Indonesia
Ceremonial textile [*tampan*]   19th century
cotton, dyes; supplementary weft weave
66.0 x 62.0 cm
Acquired through gift and purchase from the Collection of
Robert J. Holmgren and Anita Spertus, New York, 2000
2000.804

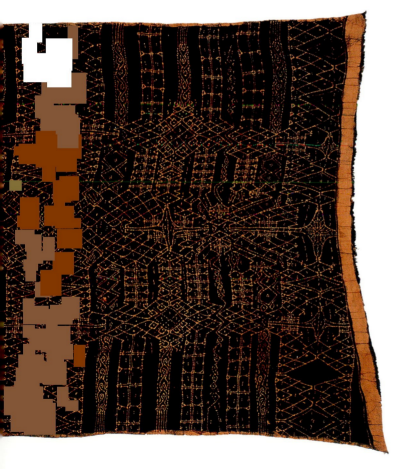

(above) Balinese people
Tenganan, Bali, Indonesia
Ceremonial cloth [*kamben geringsing patelikur isi*]   1900–1925
cotton, natural dyes; double ikat
214.0 x 39.0 cm
1980.726

(left) Java, Indonesia
Collected Bali
Ceremonial cloth   19th century
cotton, natural dyes; hand-drawn batik
92.0 x 265.0 cm
1987.1832

Balinese people
Bali, Indonesia
Shoulder or breast cloth [*selendang* or *kamben*] c. 1900
silk, dyes; weft ikat
45.0 x 230.0 cm
1989.419

Lampung, south Sumatra, Indonesia
Ceremonial textile [*kumbut juangga*]   c. 1850
silk, dyes; weft ikat
394.0 x 88.0 cm
Acquired through gift and purchase from the Collection of
Robert J. Holmgren and Anita Spertus, New York, 2000
2000.880

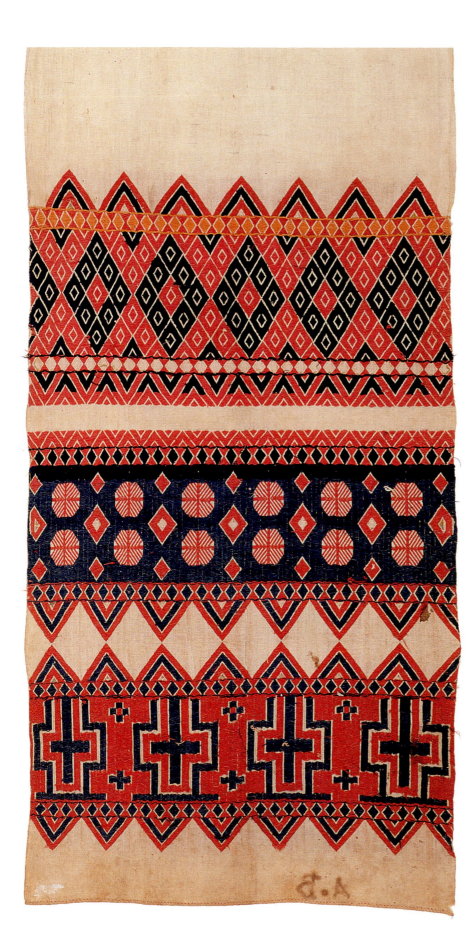

Sa'dan Toraja district, Sulawesi, Indonesia
Ceremonial loin cloth and banner [*pio uki*]   19th century
cotton, dyes; supplementary weft weave
550.0 x 46.0 cm
Acquired through gift and purchase from the Collection of
Robert J. Holmgren and Anita Spertus, New York, 2000
2000.669

Toraja people
Kalumpang district, Sulawesi, Indonesia
Ceremonial hanging and shroud [*paporitonoling*]   19th century
cotton, dyes; warp ikat
101.0 x 126.0 cm
Acquired through gift and purchase from the Collection of
Robert J. Holmgren and Anita Spertus, New York, 2000
2000.734

Endeh people
Flores, Indonesia
Man's shoulder cloth [*semba*] c. 1915
cotton, dyes; warp ikat
215.0 x 95.0 cm
Conserved with the assistance of
Mrs Dianne and Mr Gordon Johnson
Acquired through gift and purchase from the
Collection of Robert J. Holmgren and Anita Spertus,
New York, 2000
2000.747

Roti, Indonesia
Woman's skirt [*pou*]   early 20th century
cotton, natural dyes; warp ikat
60.0 x 169.0 cm
1984.1988

Paminggir people
Lampung, south Sumatra, Indonesia
Woman's ceremonial skirt [*tapis*]   19th century
silk, cotton, dyes; warp ikat, embroidery
114.0 x 128.0 cm
Acquired through gift and purchase from the Collection of
Robert J. Holmgren and Anita Spertus, New York, 2000
2000.784

Tenganan, Bali, Indonesia
Ceremonial breast cloth and sacred textile
[*geringsing petang desa cecempakan*]
1900–1925
cotton, natural dyes; double ikat
176.0 x 61.5 cm
1980.725

(above) Lampung, south Sumatra, Indonesia
Ceremonial textile [*kumbut juangga*] late 18th century
silk, bast fibre, dyes; weft ikat
196.0 x 52.0 cm
Acquired through gift and purchase from the Collection of
Robert J. Holmgren and Anita Spertus, New York, 2000
2000.877

(below) Javanese people
Surakarta, Java, Indonesia
Ceremonial skirt cloth [*kain pinarada mas*] early 20th century
cotton, natural dyes, gold leaf; batik, gold-leaf gluework
104.5 x 249.5 cm
Conserved with the assistance of Therma Quilts Pty Ltd
1987.1823

Balinese people
Bali, Indonesia
Shoulder or breast cloth [*kain cepuk*]   19th century
silk, natural dyes; weft ikat
265.0 x 80.0 cm
1984.3182

(above) Toraja people
Rongkong district, Sulawesi, Indonesia
Ceremonial head cloth and sacred heirloom [*tali tau batu*] 19th century
cotton, dyes; slit tapestry weave
289.0 x 33.0 cm
Acquired through gift and purchase from the Collection of
Robert J. Holmgren and Anita Spertus, New York, 2000
2000.715

(below) Toraja people
Rongkong district, Sulawesi, Indonesia
Ceremonial head cloth and sacred heirloom [*tali tau batu*] 19th century
cotton, dyes; slit tapestry weave
350.0 x 33.0 cm
Acquired through gift and purchase from the Collection of
Robert J. Holmgren and Anita Spertus, New York, 2000
2000.726

Gujarat, India
Traded to Sulawesi, Indonesia
Ceremonial cloth and sacred heirloom
17th–18th century
handspun cotton, natural dyes, natural mordants;
hand-drawn batik,
mordant block printing, mordant painting
506.0 x 99.0 cm
Gift of Michael and Mary Abbott 1987
1987.1077

(right) Toraja people
Rongkong district, Sulawesi, Indonesia
Ceremonial banner [*roto*]   c. 1800–1899
cotton, natural dyes; tie-dyeing, stitch-resist dyeing
417.0 x 61.0 cm
1981.1147

(far right) Toraja people
Rongkong district, Sulawesi, Indonesia
Ceremonial banner [*roto*]   19th century
cotton, natural dyes; tie-dyeing, stitch-resist dyeing
416.0 x 49.0 cm
1982.2306

Coromandel coast, India
Traded to Toraja region, Sulawesi, Indonesia
Ceremonial cloth and sacred heirloom
[*mawa* or *ma'a*]
17th–18th century (detail)
handspun cotton, natural dyes, natural
mordants; mordant painting, mordant
printing, hand-drawn batik
346.0 x 105.5 cm
Conserved with the assistance of
Maiya Keough
Gift of Michael and Mary Abbott 1987
1987.1073

Malay people
South Sumatra, Indonesia
Woman's ceremonial skirt [*kain sarong limar*]   19th century
silk, gold thread, dyes; weft ikat, supplementary weft weave
85.0 x 153.5 cm
Conserved with the assistance of Louise Williams
Acquired through gift and purchase from the Collection of
Robert J. Holmgren and Anita Spertus, New York, 2000
2000.905

Surakarta, Java, Indonesia
Skirt cloth [*kain panjang*] 20th century (detail)
cotton, dyes; hand-drawn batik
104.5 x 252.0 cm
1984.3067

KANGJENG WONOGIRI
Surakarta, Java, Indonesia
Skirt cloth [*kain panjang*] c. 1965 (detail)
cotton, dyes; hand-drawn batik
104.0 x 251.0 cm
1984.3079

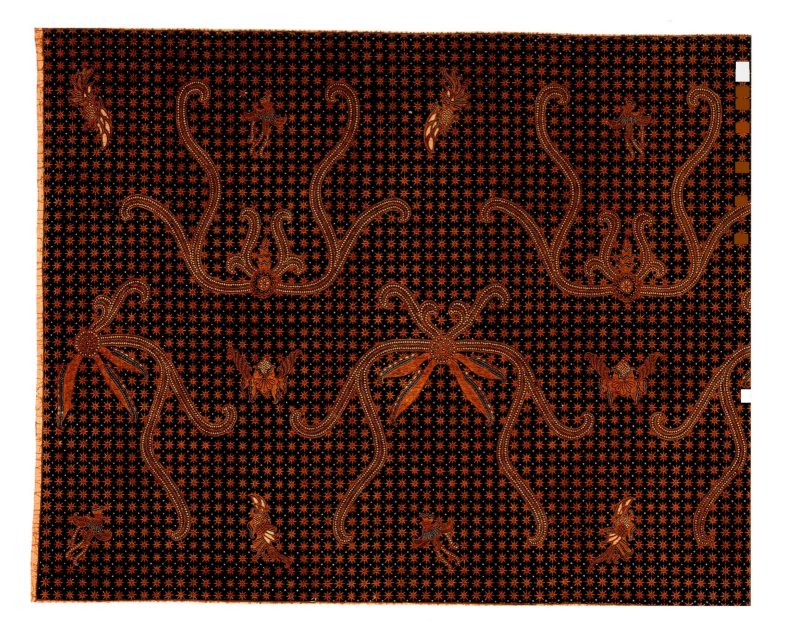

KANGJENG WONOGIRI
Surakarta, Java, Indonesia
Skirt cloth [*kain panjang*] c. 1965 (detail)
cotton, dyes; hand-drawn batik
105.0 x 252.0 cm
1984.3085

Lasem, Java, Indonesia
Skirt cloth [*kain panjang*] early 20th century (detail)
cotton, natural dyes; hand-drawn batik
105.0 x 272.0 cm
1987.1058

Peranakan Chinese community
North Java, Indonesia
Woman's skirt [*kain sarong*]   19th century
cotton, natural dyes; hand-drawn batik, hand painting
101.0 x 111.5 cm
1987.1063

Peranakan Chinese community
Cirebon or Lasem, Java, Indonesia
Woman's skirt [*kain sarong*]   late 19th century (detail)
cotton, dyes; hand-drawn batik
108.0 x 194.0 cm
Acquired through gift and purchase from the Collection of
Robert J. Holmgren and Anita Spertus, New York, 2000
2000.963

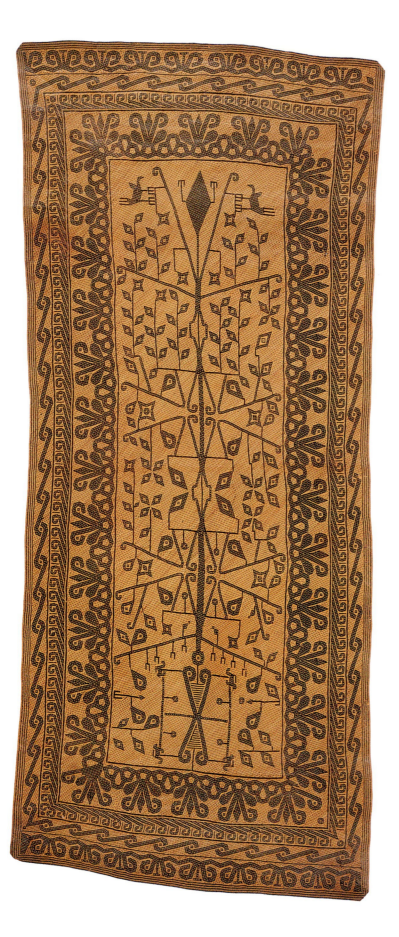

Ngaju people
Kalimantan, Indonesia
Ceremonial mat [*amak dare*]   early 20th century
bamboo, natural dyes; interlacing
205.3 x 88.8 cm
1994.1451

Peranakan Chinese community
Lasem, Java, Indonesia
Ceremonial canopy or coverlet [*lelangit*]   early 20th century
cotton, dyes; hand-drawn batik
257.0 x 209.0 cm
1984.3089

Batavia (Jakarta), Java, Indonesia
Woman's skirt cloth [*kain sarong*]   1900–1925
cotton, natural dyes; hand-drawn batik
229.5 x 105.5 cm
1981.1135

Cirebon, Java, Indonesia
Skirt cloth [*kain panjang*]   19th century (detail)
cotton, natural dyes; hand-drawn batik
98.0 x 220.0 cm
Conserved with the assistance of the Maxwell Family in memory of Anthony Forge
1989.2246

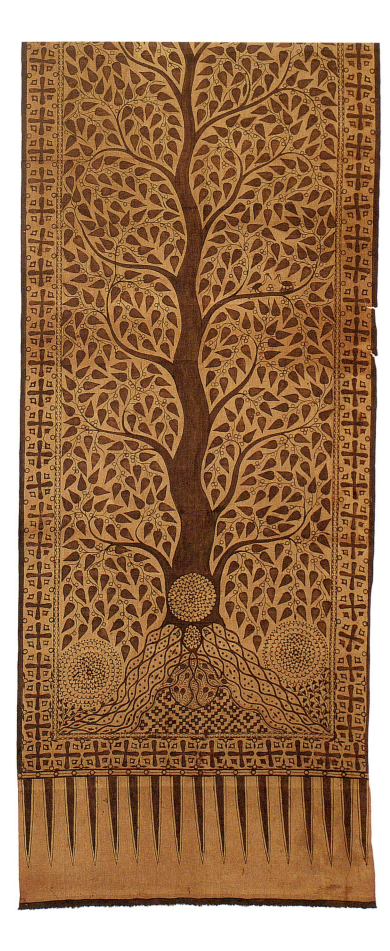

Toraja people
Sulawesi, Indonesia
Sacred heirloom textile [*ma'a* or *mawa*; *mbesa*]   early 20th century
cotton, natural dyes; painting, block printing
374.0 x 89.0 cm
1983.3684

Malay people
Jambi, Sumatra, Indonesia
Shoulder cloth [*kain batik*]   19th century
cotton, natural dyes; hand-drawn batik
226.2 x 89.4 cm
1987.1061

Coromandel coast, India
Traded to Toraja region, Sulawesi, Indonesia
Ceremonial cloth and sacred heirloom [*mawa* or *ma'a*]   early to mid 18th century
handspun cotton, natural dyes, natural mordants; mordant painting, hand-drawn batik
223.0 x 175.0 cm
Gift of Michael and Mary Abbott 1987
1987.1074

Madras, Coromandel coast, India
Traded to Sumatra, Indonesia
Ceremonial cloth and sacred heirloom [*palampore*] mid 18th century (detail)
handspun cotton, natural dyes, mordants; mordant painting, dyeing
100.2 x 293.4 cm
Conserved with the assistance of Perri Cutten
1988.1646

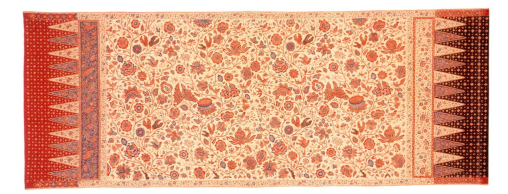

Javanese people
Lasem, Java, Indonesia
Skirt cloth [*kain panjang*]   late 19th century
cotton, natural dyes; hand-drawn batik
104.0 x 279.5 cm
1987.1059

Malay people
Palembang region, south Sumatra, Indonesia
Ceremonial shoulder cloth and sash [*kain nyulam*]   19th century
silk, natural dyes, gold thread, sequins; embroidery, appliqué, stitch-resist dyeing
83.5 x 190.0 cm
Conserved with the assistance of the Embassy of the Republic of Indonesia
1989.1495

Malay people
Komering or Palembang district, south Sumatra, Indonesia
Sampler for weaving songket brocade patterns   19th century
cotton, silk; embroidery
30.0 x 30.5 cm
Acquired through gift and purchase from the Collection of
Robert J. Holmgren and Anita Spertus, New York, 2000
2000.865.13

Lasem, Java, Indonesia
Skirt cloth [*kain panjang*]   late 19th century
cotton, natural dyes; hand-drawn batik
107.0 x 276.0 cm
1983.3693

Javanese people
Jogjakarta, Java, Indonesia
Skirt cloth [*kain panjang*]   c. 1930
cotton, natural dyes; batik
106.0 x 220.0 cm
1984.1220

Javanese people
Jogjakarta, Java, Indonesia
Skirt cloth [*kain panjang*] early 20th century
cotton, dyes; hand-drawn batik
105.0 x 252.0 cm
1984.3123

Paminggir people
Lampung, south Sumatra, Indonesia
Woman's ceremonial skirt [*tapis*]   19th century
cotton, silk, dyes; embroidery, warp ikat
130.0 x 120.0 cm
Acquired through gift and purchase from the Collection of
Robert J. Holmgren and Anita Spertus, New York, 2000
2000.800

Paminggir people
Lampung, south Sumatra, Indonesia
Woman's ceremonial skirt [*tapis inu*]   19th century
silk, cotton, natural dyes; warp ikat, embroidery
126.5 x 122.0 cm
1989.1490

Paminggir people
Lampung, south Sumatra, Indonesia
Woman's ceremonial skirt [*tapis*]   19th century
silk, cotton, dyes; supplementary weft weave, warp ikat, embroidery
122.0 x 134.0 cm
Acquired through gift and purchase from the Collection of
Robert J. Holmgren and Anita Spertus, New York, 2000
2000.783

Paminggir people
Lampung, south Sumatra, Indonesia
Woman's ceremonial skirt [*tapis*]   19th century
silk, cotton, dyes; supplementary weft weave, warp ikat, embroidery
130.0 x 120.0 cm
Acquired through gift and purchase from the Collection of
Robert J. Holmgren and Anita Spertus, New York, 2000
2000.799

Detail A

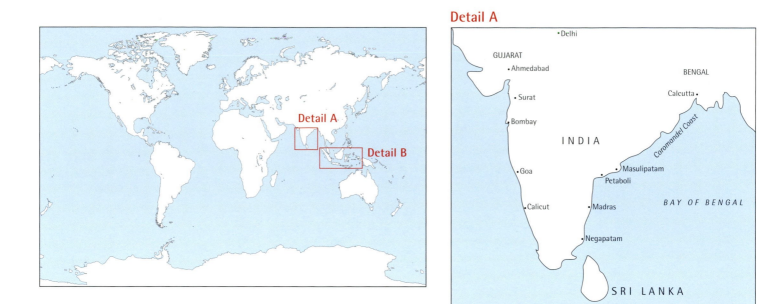

Detail B

Detailed areas of India and Indonesia